Elk & Deer

Antlered Animals of the West

tude Supe

Elk & Deer
Antlered Animals of the West

by

Kevin Van Tighem

Altitude Publishing
The Canadian Rockies / British Columbia / Colorado

Publication Information

Altitude Publishing Canada Ltd.

The Canadian Rockies / British Columbia / Colorado
Head Office: 1500 Railway Avenue
Canmore, Alberta T1W 1P6
www.altitudepublishing.com

9 8 7 6 5 4 3 2 1

Cataloging in Publication Data

Van Tighem, Kevin, 1952
Elk & Deer: Antlered Animals of the West
Includes index.
ISBN 1-55153-810-5
I.Elk--Canada, Western.2.Deer--Canada, Western. I. Title.
QL737.U55V36 2001   599.65'09712
C2001-977437-0

Printed and bound in Western Canada by Friesen Printers, Altona, Manitoba.

Altitude GreenTree Program

Altitude Publishing will plant twice as many trees as were used in the manufacturing of this product.

We acknowledge the financial support of the Government of Canada through the Book Publishing Industry Development Program (BPIDP) for our publishing activities.

Photographs
Front Cover: Bull elk by Dennis Schmidt
Back Cover: Bull moose by Dennis Schmidt & Mule deer doe by Stephen Hutchings
Frontispiece: Elk in Rocky Mountain National Park, Colorado by Gail Van Tighem
Next page: Elk at sunset by Dennis Schmidt

Project Development

Publisher	Stephen Hutchings
Design/Layout	Scott Manktelow
	Dan Klinglesmith
Editor	Dan Klinglesmith
Index	Elizabeth Bell
Financial Management	Laurie Smith

A Note from the Publisher

The world described in *Altitude SuperGuides* is a unique and fascinating place. It is a world filled with surprise and discovery, beauty and enjoyment, questions and answers. It is a world of people, cities, landscape, animals and wilderness as seen through the eyes of those who live in, work with, and care for this world. The process of describing this world is also a means of defining ourselves.

It is also a world of relationship, where people derive their meaning from a deep and abiding contact with the land—as well as from each other. And it is this sense of relationship that guides all of us at Altitude to ensure that these places continue to survive and evolve in the decades ahead.

Altitude SuperGuides are books intended to be used, as much as read. Like the world they describe, Altitude SuperGuides are evolving, adapting and growing. Please write to us with your comments and observations, and we will do our best to incorporate your ideas into future editions of these books.

Stephen Hutchings
Publisher

Contents

Acknowledgements 6

How to Use This Book. 7

Foreword. 8

The Deer Family. 11

Elk 55

Mule Deer. 89

White-tailed Deer 107

Moose 119

Caribou. 131

Afterword 134

References 136

Index 141

Author & Photographers 144

Acknowledgements

Dozens of biologists, game wardens, wildlife researchers and park officers contributed knowledge, wisdom and experience to this book. As their scribe, I hope my words do them adequate justice. Of the many people who helped me, I owe special appreciation to two in

particular, David Stalling, conservation editor of Bugle magazine, leaned over backwards to share his extensive knowledge of elk conservation. He helped me find ranchers, biologists and reserve managers to interview in Montana and Wyoming. Dave helped frame this book when I was still struggling to give it direction. Tom Beck, a biologist with the Colorado Division of Wildlife, generously helped me arrange interviews with his colleagues throughout Colorado. When Gail and I headed south on a research trip, he and his kind wife, Sandy gave our family a place to stay, fed us and helped organize our time. Tom's wisdom and clear-eyed conservation values helped me see what this book was really about. I had never met Dave Stalling or Tom Beck before starting this project.

So, to Stephen Hutchings, Sabrina Grobler, Dan Klinglesmith and the other fine people at Altitude Publishing I extend my thanks not only for making this book happen, but for these two new friends.

Thanks, also, to those who granted interviews or answered my queries: Dan Baker, Val Geist, Jim Haskins, Bob Jamieson, Marianne Moulton, Jim Olterman, Bob and Sandy Peebles, John Russell, John Seidel, Larry Simpson and Jack Ward Thomas are only a few of many. To any whose names I've missed, please forgive that oversight and accept my gratitude.

Two publications warrant recognition. Bugle magazine is one of the best conservation periodicals in North America; its back issues are a treasure trove of well-researched articles. High Country News has mounted a remarkable news archive on the World Wide Web as a free service to anyone who wants to understand the West better. Thanks to the publishers, editors and staff of both periodicals.

Mule deer in winter

Special thanks to Dr. Valerius Geist, Gail Van Tighem and David Stalling who reviewed the draft manuscript and offered helpful criticism. Any inaccuracies or failings that survived their review are my fault alone.

Lastly, to my wife and best friend Gail and our children, Corey, Katie and Brian: thanks for your patience and good humor all the evenings and weekends when I hid out with computer and research material instead of doing family things. I dedicate this book to you, and the wild creatures that so enrich our lives.

How To Use This Book

T his book is about the animals themselves, the places where they live, and the ways in which people interact with them. Deer, elk, moose and caribou—the hoofed animals of western North America—each have their own chapter with their biology, habitat, history and management.

Moose

A lookup table at the start of each chapter gives the basic facts: how big does this species get, when does it breed, where is it found. The rest of the chapter goes into depth, quoting where possible from current experts and referring to current issues.

Because of the way Altitude SuperGuides organize information, you may want to take advantage of the Index at the back to track down information scattered throughout the book on a particular subject of interest to you, whether it be predators, parasites, game ranching, hunting or national parks.

If you're interested in learning about basic things that apply to all hoofed ungulates-for example, their specialized stomachs, antlers or hooves—your first stop should be the chapter entitled "The Deer Family." If you're interested in how people and ungulates interact, check out the section "Ungulates and People." Or, if you are planning a weekend of wildlife viewing and want to know some promising locations, as well as tips on how to find ungulates and their predators, your best starting point will be "References."

As the West becomes more crowded and the world becomes more complicated, conservation of wild places and the animals that live there has never been more important. That's why this book includes sections on "Wildlife Management Agencies" and "Conservation Organizations." Your voice as a citizen conservationist can only help if you make it heard.

Lastly, "Selected Readings" offers a sampling of some of the finest books and magazines on antlered animals and their habitat currently available. It is far from comprehensive, however—a wealth of good writing awaits those who search.

Ultimately, the best way to use this book may be to spend a long day out in the wild studying tracks, watching ungulates and contemplating habitat—and then come home and browse through Elk & Deer at random. It's designed that way.

Foreword

The wind had died and fine snow wafted down the breeze as I strapped skis to my feet, waved goodbye to Gail, and began the climb through lodgepole pines to a low pass. My stomach was full, my clothing warm, and the skis sliced easily through new snow.

In the pass I cut moose tracks-deep holes punched into the snow, winding from one clump of shrubs to the next. The moose had nipped and pruned alders beside the trail, shredding stems as thick as a pencil. It had ignored a nearby buffaloberry, but thoroughly browsed an adjacent poplar sapling. From my point of view, both looked equally unappetizing.

Rounded tracks emerged from the timber, crossed the moose spoor and turned onto the ski trail. Coasting downhill on top of the cougar tracks, I wondered if the big cat had met the moose last night.

A view opened into Pass Creek valley. In summer, a popular tourist road brings hikers and picnickers to a scenic canyon near the head of this valley, but in winter a closed gate blocks traffic. Overnight, the valley becomes wilderness. The ski trail I had been following ended at the edge of the valley. Now the cougar and I had it to ourselves.

The wind had come up again. I stopped and listened to the rushing sound, like distant rapids, of air filtering through the branches of a million pines. The far mountainside was swept clean of snow except in sheltered hollows and among the stringers of timber that ribboned its contours. Spindrift plumed from the summit. Wraiths of blown snow danced crazily across the slopes. No animals showed. A raven skimmed drunkenly down the wind.

On the valley floor the snow became deeper and softer. I felt my energy begin to flag. A clutter of deer tracks showed near the edge of the trees. I angled across knowing the hardened snow would help support my weight. Dropping-littered craters showed where the deer had dug down to find juniper and green bearberry.

The deer tracks, winding apart and converging again along the edge of the forest, led me down valley. Fresh tracks joined the trail. Shortly later, the sudden flash of a white flag flickered just inside the pines. Two whitetails -- no, six -- bounded off like carousel ponies, tails flagging jauntily. The first deer stopped, framed between two trees, ears alert. She stared at me, glanced back at the others, and saw that they had veered away into dense aspens. Left alone, she flagged her tail again and leaped off in pursuit of the herd.

Not much farther along I saw a fallen log whose shape seemed strange. I put my binoculars on it: another deer, lying in her daybed. Although she faced away from me, both ears pointed backward. I took another step and she exploded from her bed. Two half-grown fawns appeared from nowhere. They vanished into the trees, bounding high at every second or third jump.

Out of the trees, the wind sandblasted me with pellet snow as I broke trail up to the abandoned road that would take me down valley and home. Something dark and blocky loomed on the mountain slope. A five-point bull elk was grazing on a wind-cleared meadow. Four more bulls lay nearby, two with heads down and antlers tilted to one side, asleep.

The road dipped into heavy aspens, then emerged into the open again. The elk had spotted me; one by one they stood up, staring. As I passed below, even though I was hundreds of yards away, they turned and stepped jerkily away, then began to lope up the slope. From time to time they stopped to watch, silhouetting themselves against the snow. I turned away, communicating as best I could that I meant no harm, but they were taking no chances. One by

Bull elk bugling

one they paused at the crest of a limber pine ridge, then disappeared over the top into the timber.

Turning a corner I stopped abruptly. On the windswept prairie below, at least 500 elk were spread out, grazing.

Finding a screen of wind-pruned Douglas fir, I hunkered down out of the wind and dug out my lunch. My sandwich was deer meat from a doe mule deer that had watched me too long one early morning last November. I chewed slowly, converting deer into human as I watched wild elk convert bunchgrass to animal flesh. The grass danced amid the oxygen we both breathed; the evening sun illuminated the world we both shared.

I would be home soon, my spirit nourished by animals whose lives I had briefly shared today; my body nourished by their meat. They would be home too–still here, in the dark and wind, watching and listening for cougars, wolves: other hunters.

The Deer Family (*Cervidae*)

Fleeing bull moose

Mountain lion, wolf and human being have a lot in common. We all, for instance, consist of grass, leaves and little green twigs. Converting green plants into bright-eyed hunters is so commonplace an alchemy we rarely give it any thought.

The magic that runs this world is so familiar that most of us are blind to it. Still, changing lead into gold could scarcely be more marvelous than to turn plants into predators. This alchemy is, to a large degree, the product of a few species of slender animals with long legs, nervous ears and lightning-fast reflexes.

Elk, mule deer, white-tailed deer, moose and caribou are among the few large animals that can convert green vegetation efficiently into animal protein. That specialty makes them important as meals for other animals—so they also

specialize in the art of avoiding predators. Those dual needs—to find and process plants as food while avoiding becoming food themselves—shape almost every attribute of these animals.

Wild ungulates are central figures in the dance of life—living links among sun, soil, and sentient life. Their trails stitch together the living landscapes of western North America—from moss-green alpine meadows down through shadowed forests of spruce and pine, across sun-baked sagelands and windy foothills, to green galleries of cottonwood

forest that follow rivers down to the sea. They know the West far better than we ever will. They live there more vividly than we ever can. Their senses—smell, hearing and vision—are unimaginably sharper than ours. They are constantly alert, run faster than we can, and never come in from the cold.

Sensitive animals, quick to respond to change, wild ungulates are intimately bonded to the places where they live. Their life cycles follow the seasons: they give birth when greenery is most lush, mate before winter's hardship saps their strength, and adjust their behavior and feeding habits to whatever each season provides. Animals that range the high country in summer commonly migrate long distances to low elevation winter haunts when the snows come.

And all the time they remain fully engaged in the age-old partnership between predator and prey.

Just as members of the deer family convert vegetation into the flesh of the predators that eat them, so do these animals shape the very vegetation itself. Where elk become over-abundant, aspen forests begin to die. Deer and moose browse the new growth from willows and serviceberries, shaping rangy shrubs into dense, hedge-like growth. Trails ter-

race the grassy slopes of heavily used winter ranges. When ungulates become too abundant for lack of predators, whole plant communities vanish, giving way to new types of vegetation. Junipers and red-osiers wither, bare soil appears, and gullies spread up the slopes. Less-palatable kinds of plants take over the threadbare landscape.

Richard Nelson, writing in Heart and Blood, Living with Deer in America—says: "...the deer is made from the world in which she lives,...this world is shaped by her existence in it, and...each is deeply infused with the other's wildness."

Familiarity breeds contempt. In many parts of the West the recent abundance of deer and elk has led people to

take wild ungulates for granted. We feed them like pets, confine them on farms, shoot them over bait—as if the wildness of their nature is no longer important to us, or them. At their best, nonetheless, these animals are the ultimate expressions of the natural, living West. Their behavior - even when bedded in a resort subdivision, raiding an orchard or strolling down a suburban alley—is the product of hundreds of centuries of natural selection. A world of hungry predators, bitter winters, drought, floods and the long stillness of the living wild has honed wild ungulates to near-perfection. Their continued wellbeing now depends, to an uncomfortable degree, on the wisdom of our choices.

Ice Age Giants

If cold climates, large continents and heavy predation pressure all tend to produce animals with large bodies, then it should be no surprise that enormous creatures ranged North America during the Pleistocene Ice Ages. Mastodons traveled south along the Rocky Mountains at least as far as Utah, where they survived until only 7,000 years ago. Saber-toothed cats and American lions hunted oversized bison and other now-extinct herbivores. The biggest deer ever known were products of the Ice Ages.

Remains preserved in deep bogs in Ireland show that the so-called Irish elk (Megaloceros) -- a giant ancestor of the fallow deer that lived in northern Europe during the Pleistocene Ice Ages -- supported antlers spanning up to 14 feet and weighing more than 100 pounds. The stag-moose

(Cervalces) lived in North America. Its antlers may have been even more massive than those of the Irish elk. Both species probably died out about 9,000 years ago.

Nineteenth century biologists fought important philosophical battles over the Irish elk. Some refused to accept a theory of evolution that included the possibility of any animal going extinct. Instead, they insisted that Irish elk either still survived somewhere or had been merely a form of moose. In reality, Irish elk were only very distantly related. Others used the Irish elk's oversized antlers as proof that animals evolved along straight lines -- in this case from a small antlered animal to progressively larger antlered animals -- until they hit a dead end. These biologists felt that Irish elk became extinct be-

cause their huge antlers became too heavy and awkward.

As biologists have continued to refine the theory of evolution and our understanding of animal behavior, a more believable interpretation has emerged. Valerius Geist thinks that Irish elk -- living in vast, lush grasslands populated by large, formidable predators -- used long-distance running as their chief escape strategy. Their survival depended on being able to find and process food efficiently into energy. Large antlers advertised bulls with just that ability to prospective mates. As forests spread and their habitat shrank, however, Irish elk could no longer sustain their extravagant lifestyle. They became vulnerable to organized human hunters -- eventually going extinct along with many other Pleistocene mega-creatures.

There may be no better way to find our own ways into a deep and lasting relationship with the West, than to follow the cloven-hoofed tracks of its wild ungulates as far as they will take us into the wild—and to contemplate what we find revealed there.

Ungulates

Taxonomists—scientists who classify living things—consider most ungulates to belong to the order Artiodactyla: hoofed animals with two or four toes. Artiodactyla includes deer, javelinas, sheep and other ungulates whose hooves are formed by two toes. Another order—the Perissodactyla - includes ungulates like elephants and horses with an uneven number of toes.

Members of the Artiodactyla subdivide into smaller groups depending on the design of their stomachs. Hippopotamus, hogs and javelinas—which have simple stomachs like ours --belong to the suborder Suidae. Another sub-order—Ruminantia—includes ungulates whose complex stomachs help them digest poor quality food such as grass and leaves. Ruminants include camels, giraffes, bison and antelopes. Only in one family of ruminants—the Cervidae—do the males grow antlers.

Elk, moose, white-tailed deer and mule deer, then, belong in the order Artiodactyla, the suborder Ruminantia, and the family Cervidae. Although all are cervids, they aren't closely related. Mule deer and whitetails are New World deer; they evolved in the Western Hemisphere long before the first of their larger relatives wandered onto North American soil. Elk, moose and caribou, which appear to have evolved originally in Eurasia, are Old World deer that only spread across North America recently - at least in geological terms.

Males of most deer species grow antlers. Females remain unadorned, except female caribou who sprout an annual set of headgear considerably more modest than the extravagant racks of their mates.

Origins

Hoofed mammals have existed on earth far longer than humans—at least 60 million years.

Deer-like ungulates—those with antlers—began to evolve about 20 million years ago in Eurasia. From there they spread west to Europe and east to North America. Whitetailed and mule deer are so unique that biologists believe their ancestors must have arrived on this continent very early in the history of the deer family—perhaps four million years ago. Spreading across the continent, the small ancestral deer gave rise to the whitetailed deer.

Whitetails are the oldest North American deer and the ancestors of both coastal black-tailed deer and mule deer. Based on genetic evidence, blacktails evolved from whitetail populations isolated

Life in the Middle

Ecologists often use the idea of the food pyramid to describe how natural systems work. The sun's energy powers most ecosystems, because plants -- at the bottom and widest part of the food pyramid -- can use sunlight to convert air and water into living matter. Plants are the most abundant form of life on Earth.

Ungulates, mice and grasshoppers are herbivores. They occupy the middle levels of the food pyramid. These animals can convert abundant plant matter into animal tissue. Because plants are so abundant, there are usually many animals nearest to the bottom of the food pyramid.

Predators, at the top of the pyramid, are least common because they feed on herbivores. Each level in the pyramid must be less abundant than the level below, or it would exhaust its food supply.

Deer and elk can become abundant because the vegetation they eat makes an abundant food supply. In temperate climates like the Rocky Mountains, however, that food supply sometimes vanishes under snow or becomes scarce because of drought or cold. Food scarcity -- even just for a few weeks - can devastate populations. On the other hand, ungulate populations recover quickly because they give birth annually and take good care of their young.

Elk and deer breed prolifically partly because they serve as food for predators; their populations need to replace frequent losses. Staying alive, then, largely centers around finding enough vegetation to eat and avoiding predators.

Woodland caribou

along the Pacific Coast one or two million years ago. The continental glaciers of the Pleistocene Ice Ages kept eastern whitetails and western blacktails separated for hundreds of thousands of years. When the ice melted back about 10,000-14,000 years ago, both species spread into the Rocky Mountains and the western edge of the prairies where they met and mated—giving rise to the newest North American deer: mule deer.

The ancestors of our modern elk appeared in Alaska about a million years ago. Stag-moose - giant relatives of the moose that are now extinct—arrived 500,000 years ago. Oceans were not as deep then as they are today. The glacier ice that carpeted most of the Northern Hemisphere contained much of the Earth's water. The Bering Sea—which even today is shallow—became dry land as those continental glaciers grew and

spread. Elk and moose were among many species, including grizzly bears, wolves and humans, that colonized North America by dispersing across the broad, shrubby hillsides of Beringia—the immense land bridge that connected Siberia to Alaska.

Northern ungulates and their predators ranged freely between the two continents until melting glaciers refilled the Bering Sea about 10,000-15,000 years ago. Ice Age glaciers, however, kept elk and moose from spreading south out of Beringia until about the same time.

Archaeologists continue to argue over when people first spread south across North America. Elk and moose had lots of experience with human predators, since these animals shared Beringia with humans. Whitetails and mule deer that lived south of the great glaciers, however, encountered their first human hunters only

10,000-15,000 years ago. Humans were not merely a new predator; their use of fire created new habitats, too—mostly ideal for herbivorous animals.

Kinds of Deer

More than 40 deer species range the earth—from northern Africa and the British Isles across Europe, Asia and throughout the Americas. Some deer live on small islands in the Pacific Ocean. Only Antarctica, Australia and central and southern Africa lack native deer of one sort or another.

Biologists often cite Bergmann's Rule, which states that the size of animals depends both on how isolated they are and how near the Equator they dwell. Small animals have a large surface area compared with their body mass, so they can get rid of heat fast. Besides, the same unit of land can feed more small animals than large ones—an important consideration when animals must occupy an island or other small space.

Large animals, on the other hand, have more body mass relative to their surface area.

This means they can conserve heat better—a useful adaptation for cold climates.

Valerius Geist, however, points out that Bergmann's Rule falls down on closer scrutiny. Geist points out that the largest ungulates are at

about a latitude of 65 degrees North; closer to the Arctic, ungulates become smaller again. Heavy predation pressure over a long time—as was the case during the Ice Ages—resulted in larger-bodied prey animals. In the absence of predation

Kinds of Deer

Genus	Species	Where found
Alces	Moose	Northern Europe, Asia and North America
Axis	Chital	Southern Asia
	Hog Deer	Southern Asia
	Bawean Deer	Asia
	Calamian Deer	Asia
Blastocerus	Marsh Deer	South America
Capreolus	Roe Deer	Europe and Asia
Cervus	Red Deer	Northern Europe and Asia
	Elk (Wapiti)	Northeastern Asia and North America
	Sambar Deer	Southern Asia
	White-lipped Deer	Tibet
	Schomburk's Deer	Thailand (probably extinct)
	Swamp Deer	India
	Thamin Deer	Southeastern Asia
	Rusa Deer	Southern Asia
	Sika Deer	Southern Asia
Dama	Fallow Deer	Europe and western Asia
Elaphodus	Tufted Deer	China
Elaphurus	Pere David's Deer	China (now extinct in the wild)
Hippocamelus	Chilean Huemel Deer	South America
	Argentinean Huemel Deer	South America
Hydropotes	Water-deer	Southeastern Asia
Mazama	Red Brocket	South America
	Brown Brocket	South America
	Little Red Brocket	South America
	Pygmy Brocket	South America
Moschus	Musk Deer	Southeastern Asia
	Siberian Musk Deer	Eastern Asia
	Szechwan Musk Deer	China
Muntiacus	Indian Muntjac	Southern Asia
	Reeve's Muntjac	Southeastern Asia
	Black Muntjac	China
	Fea's Muntjac	Southern Asia
Odocoileus	Mule Deer	North America
	Black-tailed Deer	North America
	White-tailed Deer	North and Central America
Ozotoceros	Pampas Deer	South America
Pudu	Pudu Deer	South America
Rangifer	Caribou	Northern Europe, Asia and North America

Overleaf: Bull elk grazing at airstrip, Banff National Park, Alberta

the average size of animals shrinks, as is the case with some isolated Arctic caribou herds.

Even so, deer that live on islands and in warm climates frequently are small. The smallest deer is the pudu, found in South America. Barely a foot tall, a large pudu weighs 20 pounds—less than a springer spaniel. North of the equator, the smallest deer include Florida's Key deer—a race of whitetail which lives on small tropical islands—and Arizona's Coues whitetail, another race of whitetail restricted to the "sky island" mountain ranges of the hot Sonoran desert.

Large deer species live mostly in the interior of large continents or in subarctic cli-mates. The largest is the moose, which can weigh more than half a ton—as much as 50 pudus—and towers over the tallest human. It ranges throughout the cold, forested parts of North America, Asia and Europe.

Hooves

Elk, deer, moose and caribou walk on tiptoes—on the tips of two toenails, in fact. Their distinctive two-parted tracks are the ungulate equivalent of paired fingertips.

Hooves are simply two modified toes that protrude from the end of the leg. Other toes persist as minor structures on the back of the foot, known as dewclaws. Dewclaws do not normally appear in an ungulate's track because they seldom contact the ground except when the animal is traveling over boggy ground or deep snow. Moose and caribou tracks, however, often show dewclaws in mud and snow because these snow-country and muskeg animals need to spread their weight over as much of the foot surface as possible to keep from sinking into their boggy habitats.

Ungulate legs are different from ours. What in a human would be the ball and heel of the foot are actually part of the animal's leg, not its foot. In fact, the pronounced backward-bending joint in the middle of an ungulate's hind leg is the equivalent of our heel.

Signatures in the Snow

Ungulates lead secret lives through much of the year, but winter's snow lets hunters and naturalists decode the stories of their daily travels. Of course, before you can make sense out of the story, you need to be able to figure out what kind of animal wrote it.

Mule and white-tailed deer tracks look similar, but mule deer tracks are generally larger and more elongated than those of whitetails. In wet snow or mud, a buck whitetail's track is more heart-shaped than a doe's. Doe tracks often pinch in a bit about two-thirds of the way toward the tip. In November, some hunters track rutting whitetail

Elk

Moose

bucks by looking for their distinctive, swaggering gait, with drag marks connecting their hooves.

Elk also leave drag marks when they walk in snow. Their foot-dragging gait may help explain why elk rarely winter in deep snow country: they lose too much precious energy walking. The kidney-shaped hoof tracks of elk, connected by grooves through the snow, often lead to cratered-out feeding areas.

Moose lift their feet high when walking --

Mule deer

White-tailed deer

Caribou

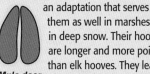

an adaptation that serves them as well in marshes as in deep snow. Their hooves are longer and more pointed than elk hooves. They leave foot drag marks only in very deep, soft snow or, when early snows coincide with the moose rut when amorous bulls swagger through the woods in search of mates.

Winter tracks reveal the tactics ungulates use to avoid predators. Fleeing ungulates often wind their way through heavy brush and then stand, listening for the sounds of pursuit. They also double back downwind of their back trails to pick up the scent of anyone who might be following.

Antlers

Antlers are the most distinctive characteristics of the deer family. Only males grow these extravagant masses of bone, except in the case of caribou where females carry undersized antlers. Bull elk and moose may bear antlers that weigh 30-65 pounds / 15-30 kilograms when fully grown—and each male grows a fresh new set each summer.

It seems impractical for an animal who eats poor quality food much of each year, copes with winter energy deficits and constantly dodges predators to waste energy on heavy, awkward decorations. Antlers must be important or natural selection would have phased them out long ago.

Valerius Geist, a noted specialist on ungulate behavioral ecology, believes that antlers -

besides serving as weapons, shields and locking organs—are important symbols of fitness that help females choose the best mates. A female deer, elk, moose or caribou must be able to find the most productive vegetation and convert it efficiently into energy. Her body needs surplus energy for her growing fetus and, after her young are born each year, to produce milk. Fast-growing fetuses and well-nourished newborns, after all, grow rapidly into fawns or calves that can outrun other animals that want to eat them.

Male deer and elk put no energy into developing young or feeding them. Instead, the most vigorous and well-adapted males divert their excess energy into growing large, showy antlers. They use those antlers as weapons to intimidate and displace other males, and as status symbols to impress females. Females usually mate with the largest antlered males. The payoff to the female is that by mating with the most extravagant male she ensures that her offspring will inherit his genetic traits. They are likely to grow rapidly, use food energy efficiently and, in the fullness of time, also become successful breeders.

Other ungulates wear elaborate headgear too. Bighorn sheep, goats, bison and members of the ox family all have horns instead of antlers. Horns grow from the base and never fall off, unlike antlers which grow from the tips and are shed each year. The pedicel (base) is the only permanent feature of a male deer or elk's antler.

Antlers

Elk
Mature bull elk have brow tines that point forward, but the main antler sweeps backward.

Mule deer
Mule deer antlers fork, and each fork branches again.

White-tailed deer
The main beam of a whitetail antler sweeps forward, with tines emerging from the top.

Moose
Moose have spreading, palmate antlers.

Caribou
Most caribou have a small, palmate "shovel" that points forward, while the main antler sweeps backward like an elk's — but the ends are palmate.

When an antler begins to grow—right about the time the first blush of green spills across the spring countryside—cells called osteoblaths congregate at the pedicel. No other cells can multiply and grow as fast as osteoblaths. They deposit cartilage at the growing end of the antler so fast that an elk or moose can grow a third of a pound of new antler each day. A 50-pound moose antler, for example, takes barely four months to develop.

As the antler grows, soft bony tissue replaces the cartilage. Velvet—a furry coating with a network of large arteries that bring blood to the antler surface—covers the whole antler. The blood is full of phosphorus, calcium and other minerals originally stored in the animal's skeleton. These minerals convert soft cartilage into hard, mature antlers.

Growing antlers require so much calcium and phosphorus, so quickly, that soon after the new antlers sprout a male ungulate develops osteoporosis (brittle bones). Broken legs or other bone injuries are a real risk. Males with growing antlers move little and spend a great deal of their time eating mineral-rich greenery. By the time the antlers are full-grown, however, the animal's bones are hard and strong again.

Antlers stop growing when the animal's testosterone supply drops in late summer. The velvet coating on the outside of the antlers loses its blood supply and dies in response to changing hormone levels. It dries and begins to peel off. The animal gets rid of the tattered strips of velvet by rubbing his antlers vigorously on small trees and shrubs. Antler rubbing often kills the tops of the plants. Sap and plant juices react with blood stains on the antlers in a chemical reaction that produces the characteristic brown color on all but the smooth tips of an ungulate's antlers. According to David Petersen—author of Racks: The Natural History of Antlers and the Animals that Wear Them—the distinctive grooves and ridges that pattern ungulate antlers are the

Antler Harvesting

An army of hopeful antler collectors spreads out across Montana's Sun River Game Refuge each year on May 15. Most wintering elk and mule deer are long-gone but their antlers remain behind, waiting for collectors to convert them to cash. Farther south, Boy Scouts conduct an annual antler collecting blitz in the National Elk Refuge near Jackson Hole, Wyoming. Though not nearly so lucrative as the velvet antler trade, cast antlers still bring in ready money. Collectors earn up to $10 dollars a pound for mediocre antlers and much more for good matched specimens. In the annual Jackson Hole auctions, symmetrical matched sets fetch as much as $2,000 USD. Some years, Jackson Hole's Scouts gross close to $50,000 USD for up to 7,000 pounds of antlers. The scouts give most of

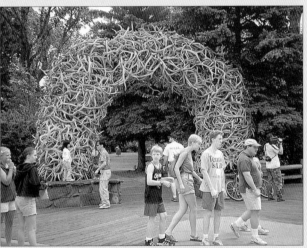

Elk antler arch, Jackson Hole, Wyoming

their profits back to the National Elk Refuge to pay for winter elk feed, pocketing the rest to support scouting activities.

Elsewhere, antler collecting is a purely commercial endeavor with little conservation payback. Some antler collectors make up to USD $15,000 a year, supplementing seasonal backwoods employment in places such as northern British Columbia.

tracks of blood vessels that ran along the antlers when they were still growing. Fully grown antlers are essentially dead, since they have no blood supply, marrow or nerve supply.

Male ungulates display their antlers—and their body profiles—as much to avert the need for a fight as to provoke

one. They stretch out their necks and show their size in profile, parading past one another. Usually, smaller-antlered males give way. Actual fights are uncommon. Most take place between males with antlers of similar size. Friendly shoving matches are more common, especially before the rut. Like many weapons, the value of antlers lies partly in the fact that showing them off reduces the

likelihood of having to use them.

One advantage of growing new antlers every year is that the size of the antlers clearly reflects the animal's current level of fitness. Young males and very old males have smaller antlers than prime-aged, vigorous males. So, although growing antlers might seem a waste of metabolic energy, it actually pays off by

Vanishing Antlers

Castoff antlers litter the Western landscape by the thousands each spring. Instead of accumulating into growing piles, however, they quickly vanish. Some end up in the hands of human antler collectors. Most, however, sharpen the teeth and strengthen the skeletons of countless millions of mice, voles, squirrels and porcupines.

Deer commonly chew castoff antlers too, as well as the bones of old skeletons. Animals gnaw antlers and bones to exploit a source of concentrated calcium, phosphorus and other minerals. Natural recycling ensures that few shed antlers last more than three or four years.

"I Use Antlers in All of My Decorating"

Moose antler chandelier

Hunters hang the racks of their kills on recreation room walls in honor of memorable hunts, and memorable animals. Antlers find their ways into human homes in

various other ways too - tangible signs of the age-old bond between human and wild ungulate. A uniquely North American folk art expresses itself in chandeliers, coat racks, armchairs and even bookcases built from antlers. Summer cottages often have cribbage boards made from deer antler. Some artisans not only assemble furnishings from antlers, but carve figures and scrimshaw patterns into the antlers too.

Antler Poaching

Unlike game preserves, national parks strictly prohibit antler collecting. Castoff antlers can be important sources of calcium and other minerals for rodents such as mice and ground squirrels. The ecological value of shed antlers is just one reason that national park rangers and wardens enforce regulations prohibiting people from collecting them. National parks -- unlike places where hunting removes many male animals each fall before they can shed their antlers -- can be particularly at-

tractive to antler poachers because of the abundance of large antlers on winter ranges.

Park rangers and wardens deter antler poachers by drilling holes in antlers, painting them, or simply posting winter ranges with signs that ban antler collecting. When antler poachers choose to flout the law, penalties can be severe. Canadian national park regulations, for example, allow fines up to $25,000 CDN for poachers caught with any part of an elk.

The World Wildlife Fund and international wildlife enforcement agencies believe that the international trade in antlers has little impact on wild animals. Because ungulates produce antlers each year, shed antler collection has no impact on the animals that produce them. Nearly all velvet antlers harvested in the United States and Canada comes from farmed deer, not from deer poached solely for their velvet antler.

Ungulates in Art

The earliest known paintings by human beings feature images of deer. Cro-Magnon hunter-gatherers occupied southern France at least 15,000 years ago. They painted stylized images of mammoths, woolly rhinos and red deer on cave walls, using paints derived from ocher, ash and other natural substances. Protected from the elements, the early artwork survives today to offer tantalizing glimpses into the lives and culture of our far-distant ancestors.

More recent aboriginal art – for instance by the Ancestral Puebloans of the American southwestern deserts - also includes renderings of wild ungulates. Hunting peoples may have relied on their art to give them greater influence over animals upon whom they relied for food and clothing. The drawings may have helped to pass on cultural knowledge or sacred stories. The scribblings might have been an early form of doodling. Nobody really knows.

Art reflects how we experience and value the world, and how we perceive ourselves within it. Primitive art often showed animals being hunted, reflecting the central importance of the hunt to those cultures. Romantic artists of the 19th century showed noble stags and depraved wolves, reflecting a human-centered view of nature that attached human virtues and vices to different creatures. Wealthy colonial sport hunters of the late 19th and early 20th centuries often sought out paintings that celebrated trophy-class animals in dramatic wilderness settings. Such paintings celebrated the last wilderness fron-

tiers, the last great animals and the lasting egos of men who could afford both to seek out and exploit those places, and to commission expensive paintings.

Carl Rungius was among several painters, including Richard Freese and Friedrich Kuhnert, whose art grew out of the frontier infatuation with wilderness and trophy animals. Born in Germany, Rungius was already in his late twenties when he came to North America. He came to know the Rocky Mountains intimately. An avid hunter, Rungius often strung up his prey in lifelike poses and painted portraits of them on the spot. Most of his paintings contained at least one trophy animal posed broadside, as a hunter would hope to see it. His paintings – in spite of his post-expressionist love of paint – foreshadowed the intense realism of many late 20th century artists. In some of his latest – and best – works he became one of the first wildlife artists to turn the relationship of the wildlife subject away from the human and into its environment.

Increasingly, the most powerful wildlife art does just that. Animals stand with their backs to the viewer or half-obscured by foliage, engaged in some unseen interaction. Massive antlers no longer dominate the image. Many modern wildlife artists focus on the inter-relatedness of animal and its environment, creating images that draw the human viewer into that relationship. Modern wildlife art celebrates ungulates inside nature rather than as objects of human ambition or expressions of human values.

Moose, Upper Ram River Valley (oil on canvas) by Carl Rungius 1935

Mule deer bucks locking antlers

protecting old and young males from dangerous fights.

Prime breeding-age males are not so lucky; an aggressive deer or elk may collect as many as 50 puncture wounds from adversaries each fall.

Rumens

Grass and wood do not digest very well. Deer, elk and moose are members of the suborder

Velvet Antlers and Alternative Medicine

Koreans, Chinese and other southeast Asians have used antler velvet for at least 2,000 years as a source of healing and health. Traditional oriental medicine claims that antler velvet improves a patient's yang—an important element of an individual's spiritual and physical balance.

Some critics dismiss claims that ground up velvet antlers can cure infertility, hasten wound healing, reduce blood pressure and boost energy. However, there seems little doubt that antler velvet does have therapeutic value. The velvet covering of a growing antler is rich in blood vessels that feed calcium and other substances to the fast-growing interior of the antler. Some Russian athletes use an antler extract called Pantosine to improve performance; clinical trials suggest that another extract—chondroitin sulfate—may reduce heart attack risk.

Captive, farm-raised elk, deer and reindeer supply most of the velvet antler to the market for medicinal antler products. Deer farmers saw off the growing antlers while the velvet covering is alive and full of blood—a messy and traumatizing experience for the animal. After freezing the antlers or soaking them in alcohol, processors then slice them into thin discs and ship them to market. Some users make a hot tea or broth from the antler discs; others grind them up and use the powder in pills or effusions.

Antler velvet was once a rare and expensive commodity that only wealthy Chinese and Kore-ans could afford. The market for farmed velvet antlers skyrocketed in recent decades as southeastern Asia's economic growth produced a thriving middle class—more people who could afford expensive specialties. Researchers report that in the Korean market alone, sales skyrocketed from around 5,500 pounds / 2,500 kilograms of antler a year in the early 1970s to well more than 440,000 pound / 200,000 kilograms by the late 1990s.

North American deer farms produce more than 66,000 pounds / 30,000 kilograms of dried velvet antler with a market value of $12 million USD each year. Deer farmers now promote their products in many parts of the world as an alternative to mainstream western medicine.

Ruminantia, which gets its name from a unique series of stomachs that enable these ungulates to eat poor-quality food like dry grass. Ruminants can process their food a lot longer simply by virtue of their extended series of stomachs. Even so, they probably could not make a living from vegetation if their specialized stomachs were not also seething with special bacteria and protozoa that help them digest their food.

The rumen—where these microbes are most abundant—is the first of four stomachs through which food must pass before reaching the intestines. When ruminants eat a meal of grass or leaves, the mass of vegetation stops in the first stomach where churning stomach muscles mix it with microbes and digestive juices. After feeding, the animal finds a safe place to bed down, regurgitates the green cud into its mouth, and chews it up thoroughly before swallowing it again.

As the mixture passes progressively from one stomach to another, the bacteria break it down, releasing proteins, starches and other substances until all that remains are fine fragments of indigestible lignin and other material. This, packed tightly into blocky chunks, ends up deposited in compact piles shortly after the animal gets up to move on again.

Elk and deer have to process a lot of vegetation to stay alive, so they leave a lot of piles of droppings, or pellets, behind. Biologists sometimes count pellet piles to judge how abundant deer or elk are. It's less fun than counting the animals that deposited them, but more reliable: animal droppings don't run and hide.

Living with Predators

Ever since ungulates first appeared out of the mists of evolutionary time, other animals have hunted them. Over millions of years, predation has constantly weeded out those deer and elk most poorly suited for survival, producing today's highly-tuned survival specialists.

Reconfigured Mule Deer

Since the primary source of the body's testosterone is the testicles, testicle injuries can slow the rate of antler growth or result in deformed, twisted antler growth.

"Edwin Carter tells me that the cowboys of Routt and Rio Blanco counties in Colorado got the idea that they could improve the quality of their venison by castrating large numbers of bucks. In the spring round-up of 1891 or thereabouts they castrated every Blacktail [mule deer] fawn they could find, and there were many. The only known result was that in the years that followed some extraordinary freak antlers were seen among the Blacktail."

Ernest Thompson Seton, 1909. **Life-histories of Northern Animals**

Velvet at the Games

Steroid scandals have some athletes searching for drug-free ways to develop a winning edge in the highly profitable world of national and international sports competition. The University of Alberta recently tested 10 college football players and 27 local police officers to see if elk velvet might do the trick. Each subject took six capsules of elk velvet a day, while researchers measured their muscle mass and endurance. Announcing the study, Dr. Brian Fisher of the university's Physical Education faculty said that elk velvet contains high concentrations of 17 amino acids, including two that human bodies cannot manufacture for themselves. He hoped antler velvet would improve athletic performance and help strained muscles heal faster.

When results from the first blood test came in, however, Dr. Fisher had to take the football players off the pills. Although there was no improvement in their measured strength or endurance, they had five to six times the normal amount of testosterone -- a male sex hormone -- in their blood. Anabolic steroids produce a similar increase in testosterone. Since sports organizations test athletes for evidence of steroid use, the research subjects risked being disqualified from further competition. University authorities played it safe by canceling the research.

An inattentive deer, unhealthy elk or short-sighted moose rarely lives long. Natural selection - the constant weeding out of inferior individuals by hungry predators—has given deer and elk exceptional abilities to detect sounds and scents. They are almost constantly alert. Long legs and lean musculature let them flee quickly when danger approaches.

Ungulates have also evolved behavior patterns to cope with predators. A herd of elk or deer usually has a few individuals watching and listening while others feed. Deer and elk feed for brief periods, then lie still to chew their cuds and digest. Lying still, their senses are primed for danger while they remain hidden from hunters. Preferred bedding areas offer good visibility and several escape routes.

A deer, elk or moose chased by a four-legged predator will often flee downhill toward water. Once in a lake or large stream it has an advantage since its long legs enable it to fight back. Wolves and coyotes often wait on dry land for their prey to leave the water, but rarely try to force the attack where the footing is unsure. The instinct that leads deer and elk to flee into water can work against them in winter, however. An ungulate on ice is easy pickings for large predators. If it takes shelter in near- freezing water hypothermia can eventually weaken it to the point where its pursuers can pull it down and drag it to the water's edge.

Some human hunters resent mountain lions, wolves and coyotes as competition for

Grizzly bears hunt for elk calves in spring

a limited resource. However the very attributes we most value in our prey—intelligence, watchfulness, speed and grace—arose from countless interactions with those same predators. Without predators, diseases such as brucellosis and chronic wasting disease flourish. If it were not for the wolf, the elk and moose would not be the magnificent animals we know today. The mule deer is, to a large degree, a product of the cougar. The white-tailed deer's remarkable elusiveness was shaped, in part, by thousands of years of Native American hunting.

Mountain Lion

Mountain lions, or cougars, specialize in hunting deer, but large males easily kill prey as large as elk. Biologists in Alberta's Sheep River Valley found that some males even killed moose regularly. The big cats hunt by stalking close, then springing from cover and gripping their prey around the

neck or back, biting through the throat or backbone or simply snapping the spine.

Mountain lions have relatively small lungs and cannot run prey down. A deer that can dodge away fast has a good chance of escaping. Even if the cat manages to land on its prey the attack may still fail if the deer or elk can shake it off or knock it against a tree. I once saw a wide-eyed mule deer standing waist deep in the Bow River near Lake Louise. Fresh scrape marks along its back showed how close it had come to becoming a cougar's dinner.

When a mountain lion kills a deer or elk, it drags the body into a sheltered location and feeds. Then it covers the carcass with grass, leaves or other material to hide it from scavenging birds. The lion returns periodically to feed until the carcass is gone or another predator steals it. Like other cats, mountain lions feed by peeling the meat from the

Wolves test the health of ungulates through chasing

bones. Their jaws are too weak to crack long bones, unlike bears and members of the dog family who often break bones and eat the marrow. On a cougar kill some bones may look almost polished by the time the cat has finished stripping the meat from them.

Bears

A bear spends most of its waking hours looking for high energy food. Few meals offer quite so rich a reward as fresh venison. Bears have some of the equipment they need to be good predators too: uncannily sharp noses, high intelligence and powerful bites. However, black and grizzly bears are both built for low-speed foraging. Few bears actively hunt ungulates; it's just too much work. Instead they eat vegetation, insects and whatever they can find that is already dead. Bears commonly visit ungulate winter ranges early in the spring, looking for carrion.

Some bears become good at finding newborn elk, moose or deer. Grizzlies will sometimes hunt elk calving areas, coursing back and forth like bird dogs as they test the breeze for the faint traces of hidden calves. Other times, a grizzly may try to scatter an elk herd and isolate calves from their mothers. One Alaska study found that a few black bears had become so effective as moose calf predators that they actually reduced the moose population. By mid June, however, few bears bother trying to capture nimble young ungulates anymore.

Wolf and Coyote

Wolves and coyotes are uniquely important to the ungulates they hunt because they constantly test and chase potential prey. In doing so, they quickly find and kill unhealthy animals. This testing behavior makes them far more effective at reducing disease in ungulate herds than other hunters such as cougars and humans who simply kill the unwary. It also continually selects for alertness, speed and agility in their prey.

Wolves normally hunt in packs. A pack of wolves travels almost constantly, watching and testing the wind for any sign of potential prey. Upon detecting a prospective meal, they move in as close as they can, then give chase. Usually, the chase ends in failure. Often enough, however, one or more wolves manage to grasp the fleeing animal by its throat or

Partners for Life

Ungulates and bacteria doubtless have no real awareness of one another, but their unconscious partnership has worked well for millions of years. As long as the ungulate survives, its rumen bacteria have plenty of food and a warm, wet place to live. As long at the bacteria survive, the elk or deer can digest food that would simply bloat and kill it otherwise. It's an efficient system.

In winter, rumen bacteria offer their hosts an important added benefit. Just as compost piles generate heat as bacteria rot the compost, so does the food fermenting inside an ungulate's stomach produce heat. Those elk or deer bedded in the snow at 40° below zero look pitiably cold. The bacteria in their bellies, however, are pumping out heat that helps warm the big animals from within, saving precious metabolic energy.

leg and pull it off balance long enough for other wolves to drag it down. While wolves are effective predators, they are just as likely to steal a cougar's kill or scavenge a carcass of an animal that died of other causes.

Some coyotes hunt deer fawns in spring, but otherwise they usually leave large ungulates alone until snow carpets the winter ranges. Then small packs of coyotes begin to test wintering deer herds. From time to time, they single out an easy-to-kill fawn or other vul-

nerable animal up to the size—rarely—of a cow elk.

Biologists agree that neither wolves nor coyotes select only the weak or sick, as some people believe. They simply kill animals they can catch. Frequently these are inexperienced young animals or weakened ones, but sometimes they are healthy animals that just got unlucky. Regardless, frequent encounters with coyotes or wolves keep deer, elk and moose alert and fit, and quickly remove sick animals from the herds.

Bobcat

Bobcats may seem like small animals, but a large male bobcat can kill mule deer. In some parts of the West, deer are an important food for male bobcats. Bobcats, in fact, can sometimes be so good at killing newborn fawns that they slow down the growth of local herds. Bobcats hunt like cougars, traveling quietly through the landscape until they smell or see potential prey, then stalking close before launching a short, dashing attack.

Bambi

Whitetail fawn

"Man is in the Forest!" Walt Disney's famous animated movie Bambi helped shape the attitudes of generations of children toward both nature and hunting. The movie's animators designed the movie for emotional impact -- giving Bambi oversized dark eyes and showing the hunters as shadowy figures who killed everything in their path. Years after they first saw the movie, many people can still recall the desola-

tion that filled them in the famous scene where Bambi realizes that his mother is dead, shot by a hunter. Historian Ralph Lutts, in a 1992 essay about the impact of Bambi on American perception of nature, criticized the movie for portraying an unreal world where skunks and deer are friends, man is always evil, fire kills, and animals are simply cute little people. "The film motivates," he wrote, "but does not educate.

It may stimulate action, but not understanding."

Disney's movie was based on a novel by Austrian writer Felix Salten. The original novel remains a classic work of nature interpretation. It is far more realistic and less manipulative than the movie. Salten's deer lived in fear of hunters and killing, too, but Salten appears to have meant no moral judgment against predators. He merely tried to show how it might feel to be an animal that other creatures kill and eat.

Unlike the commercial movie, Salten's original portrayal of a deer's world was sometimes remarkably insightful: "*...the dry leaves lie on the ground, and when a foot stirs them they rustle. Then someone is coming. O, how kind last year's leaves are! They do their duty so well and are so alert and watchful. Even in mid-summer there are a lot of them hidden beneath the undergrowth. And they give warning in advance of every danger.*"

Moose lift their legs high to make travel in snow easier

Deer reduce risk to their fawns by wandering off by themselves to give birth, and leaving newborn fawns hidden until they are large and strong enough to flee from predators. The hiding strategy of young fawns is the product of many generations of bobcats and other predators who ate baby deer that failed to remain hidden and still.

Living with winter

Winter is the ultimate test for a grazing animal. Deep snow makes travel difficult. Cold temperatures cost the animals precious energy, since their bodies must burn extra fat to keep warm. Adding to the energy deficit, food is hard to find when covered by snow and most winter forage is of poor quality since green leaves are rare.

The slow, losing race against starvation and exposure means that most ungulates begin to lose weight in December and by April have almost no fat left on their bodies. Spring's first greenery usually arrives in time to save most, at least of those populations that winter on healthy range. Late snowmelt or severe spring storms, however, can spell disaster on overgrazed winter ranges.

Snow troubles moose less than it does the smaller ungulates. The same long legs and large hooves that help moose navigate wetlands and log-strewn forests in summer enable them to move with relative ease through deep snow. Moose eat mostly the buds and young twigs of trees and shrubs in winter - a food supply that rarely vanishes beneath snow pack. As a result, moose can linger in the deep snow country of the high

Deer Need Enemies

"... I have lived to see state after state extirpate its wolves. I have watched the face of many a newly wolfless mountain, and seen the south-facing slopes wrinkle with a maze of new deer trails. I have seen every edible bush and seedling browsed, first to anemic desuetude, and then to death...

"I now suspect that just as a deer herd lives in mortal fear of its wolves, so does a mountain

live in mortal fear of its deer. And perhaps with better cause, because while a buck pulled down by wolves can be replaced in two or three years, a range pulled down by too many deer may fail of replacement in as many decades..."

Aldo Leopold, 1949
"Thinking like a mountain" in
A Sand County Almanac

Birth Control for Elk

Dan Baker is a soft-spoken scientist who clearly enjoys his work at the Colorado Division of Wildlife's research facility near Fort Collins. His research subjects include about 100 hand-raised elk, deer, pronghorns and bighorn sheep. Over the years, they have taught him about chronic wasting disease, ungulate nutrition and food preferences. Most recently, they have been helping him figure out how to keep hoofed animals from having babies.

"We started the work here two or three years ago," he says. "It's not an immunocontraceptive we're testing. It's a hormonal toxin. No one else has ever worked on it before...It actually sterilizes the animal—you give the animal one injection and it's sterilized for life. It controls the release of reproductive hormones that control ovulation in females and spermatogenesis in males."

Dan Baker with elk at Fort Collins

Dr. Baker's facility is not the only one looking for ways to control ungulate birthrates. Nature's way of controlling deer and elk populations is to kill the surplus, either through starvation, disease or predation. Many small game reserves and densely settled regions, however, have no wild predators.

Local residents don't like to see animals starve, and won't tolerate human hunters—either for philosophical or public safety reasons. Lacking a natural solution, birth control seems an attractive alternative to some.

Dr. Jay Kirkpatrick, a researcher at Zoo Montana in Billings, has tested immunocontraceptives on tule elk at Point Reyes National Seashore in California. His technique tricks the elk's immune system into attacking fertilized eggs. Like allergy shots, however, immunocontraceptives have to be administered once or twice a year. This obliges reserve managers to find and isolate each cow elk repeatedly -- not easy. Since the contraceptives are delivered by shooting a dart into the elk, managers risk hitting an artery or vital organ and killing her.

The technique being tested in Colorado -- if it proves effective -- will permanently sterilize the elk. That would avoid the problem of booster shots. However, the sterile elk would no longer act normal during rutting season, possibly creating an entire new set of problems. Elk or deer herds managed through contraception will no longer act natural.

"Bulls would ignore females that are treated with it," says Dr. Baker. "You'd have a small proportion of the population that's breeding...But it will change the behavior of a female because she won't go through an estrous. So it has limitations. I think any of these fertility control agents are best for isolated populations behind fences or with some natural barriers. Otherwise it's going to take a huge effort to treat enough animals to keep the population in check."

Conservation writer Ted Kerasote feels that contraception has a role to play. However, he argues that we are looking at the wrong animals: "We are the overabundant species, not wildlife, and until we face squarely the issue of our own birth control, all forms of wildlife control...will dominate the discussion, clouding the real issue and its real solution."

mountains long after deer and elk have to move to friendlier terrain.

When snow becomes more than a foot and a half deep, deer and elk can no longer step through it. Instead, they have to force their chests against the snow like snow plows—hard, energy-wasting work. In heavily forested areas, wintering ungulates can avoid deep snows by remaining in heavy timber where the forest canopy traps a lot of snow before it can reach the ground. Food is scarce under heavy forest, however, so most deer and elk that summer at high elevations in the Rockies mi-

grate in winter to lower elevations, windy places or south-facing slopes where little snow accumulates.

Migration

In spring and summer, elk and mule deer often migrate to higher elevations, following the greenup and taking advantage of a continuous supply of highly nutritious foods. Their summer migration opens vast areas of habitat and allows them to spread out across the landscape. This reduces competition for food and makes it harder for predators to find their scattered prey.

Winter snows force mule

deer and elk to abandon the high country and migrate to places - usually at lower elevations—where the snow normally remains shallow. Moose migrate between seasonal habitats too, but rarely cover the same distances that deer and elk might. White-tailed deer are the least migratory of western ungulates.

Some migration routes are long and complicated, with mule deer and elk crossing one or even two mountain ranges during their trek to and from winter ranges. When humans build irrigation reservoirs, highways or high fences across these centuries-old migration routes, the result can be disaster for ungulates no longer able to travel safely from one seasonal home to the other. No less devastating is the ongoing conversion of winter ungulate ranges into ranchettes, tract housing and resorts.

Deer Hair Flytying

Deer hair flies

Anglers who tie their own fishing flies are always on the lookout for new materials to fool trout into thinking a hook is edible. In the 1960s some Montana flytiers began to experiment with deer hair. Hollow ungulate hairs flare when flytying thread crushes them against the shaft of a hook. A large clump of deer hair, spun around a hook and

trimmed to shape, makes a buoyant and lightweight head for a grasshopper or—when weighted—a sculpin imitation. Elk hair flares less dramatically than deer, so flytiers often use it for the wings and heads of caddis fly imitations. The tips of moose hair work well for imitating mayfly tails or the delicate legs of insect nymphs.

Hollow hair

Elk, deer and moose have three layers of insulation to get them through the winter. Thick coatings of hard fat, just beneath the skin, offer the first layer. As winter's slow starvation progresses, however, this layer gradually disappears.

Dense wool-like hair coats the outside of the animal's skin. Protruding from this, a heavy coat of long, tubular hairs forms the outer layer. These outer hairs are stiff and hollow, offering both insulation and protection from wind. By intercepting snow, hoarfrost and rain, they also help to keep the underlying wool dry.

Ungulates and People

Ancient Economies

Piles of rocks along alpine ridges in Colorado's Rocky Mountains National Park offer clues about how people lived and hunted in the days before firearms and modern technology. Although no oral tradition survives among modern Ute and Cheyenne, archaeologists have deduced that the remains were used for drive lanes. Native Americans forced herds of bighorn sheep and mule deer ahead of them, confining the retreating animals between strategically placed piles of rocks that concealed other hunters who showed themselves whenever their quarry

looked likely to move out of the drive lane. At length, they drove their prey into enclosures or defiles where hunters could kill them with spears or arrows.

Many tribes used variations of this hunting technique.

Deer were—and in many cases still are—important to aboriginal economies. Their hides—scraped, beaten and cured with a concoction of brain, ashes or other substances—provided clothing and tepee covers. Some tribes preferred elk hide to bison for footwear, because it stands up better to wear. Leg bones, broken carefully, provided sharp, rigid awls and digging tools. The antlers, too, were useful

for making tools.

North American tribes hunted deer and elk in various ways, depending partly on the nature of the local landscape. Unlike the high mountain Ute of northern Colorado, other tribes sometimes ran down elk, forced herds into deep snow, or stalked and killed them with arrows or spears. Archaeological sites in the Canadian Rockies have few elk or deer remains. It appears that either elk and deer were rare - a likely explanation, especially since winter snows were deeper during the so-called Little Ice Age that ended in the mid 1800s—or the tribes who lived there preferred moose, sheep and bison.

Deer were more abundant

Bit Players

In ceremonies portraying one Navajo emergence myth, the masked gods (yei) create First Man and First Woman by placing two ears of corn under a buckskin. Wind arrives then, and as Mirage People circle four times around the buckskin the corn becomes human. In this way humans emerge from that which feeds them.

Deer and elk, however, appear in native myth rarely compared with more powerful animal figures. Even then, they usually warrant only passing mention as food animals or characters who simply appear long enough to get a hunter lost or injured before he goes on to interact with one of the powerful beings.

Native myth rarely accorded elk and deer mythic status like

coyote, wolf, bear, raven or even rabbit. Still, traditional native beliefs demand respect of their prey by hunters. Wasting part of an ungulate -- or failing to honor its sacrifice -- risks having the animals turn against their hunters and cease to offer themselves as food. This traditional reverence, unfortunately, has been lost among some modern hunters.

Respect Those Who Feed You

We ran into plenty Injun signs...made by Salish Injuns who came here to hunt elk, as there were a number of elk toes left by the [women] hanging in branches from the limbs of the trees. The Injuns, being superstitious, say that if they waste any of the meat of any of the deer tribe, they will know this and be mad at them, and will not let them kill

them, and the Injuns will have to go hungry.

In the summer months they kill only for their immediate use, and in their fall hunts enough to dry, to bring them through the winter. The women leave only the hair of the hides they tan on the ground, and carefully tie all the hoofs of the deer tribe in small bundles and hang them up

on the limbs of trees, for the deer to see that they have used everything except their hair on the ground and their feet and horns in the trees.

Andrew Garcia, *Tough Trip Through Paradise* (describing an 1878 journey through western Montana with In-who-lise, his Nez Perce wife)

The Hunter-Conservationist

A young hunter in elk country, western Alberta

It was not recreational or subsistence hunting that nearly eradicated North America's native ungulates—for the most part, it was commercial markets for ungulate meat and hides. Once laws eliminated those markets, populations recovered. Licensed hunting of game for private use has never caused any animal species to become endangered. In fact, a small group of hunter-conservationists played a key role in restoring elk, deer and moose from the excesses of the market-hunting era.

In the early 1900s, wealthy men of influence such as William Hornaday, Theodore Roosevelt, George Bird Grinnell, C. Gordon Hewitt and Clifford Sifton formed organizations — the Audubon Society, Boone and Crockett Society and Canadian Conservation Commission— to push for an end to market-hunting and better protection for wildlife populations. William Hornaday, reflecting on frontier North America's progressive eradication of game and fur animals, wrote: "There is no such thing as safety for any wild creature, save under man's own laws."

Elite conservationists of the early 20th century used their power and influence to stop the trade in animal parts, establish closed seasons, and push for new government agencies to enforce laws and protect game.

In the 1930s, however, the vastly greater number of working class, rural and other hunters added another important piece to the conservation puzzle. Working through their hunting and fishing clubs, U.S. hunters came to a remarkable agreement: to provide money for wildlife and habitat, they would voluntarily accept a new tax on guns, fishing gear and other outdoor supplies. The Federal Aid in Wildlife Restoration Act—better known as Pittman-Roberts for its original legislative sponsors - came into effect in 1937. Since then, it has poured billions of dollars into wildlife restoration and habitat development. Pittman-Roberts imposes a mandatory tax on hunting and fishing supplies. The money generated from that tax—along with matching monies from the Federal government—goes to State wildlife agencies for projects that benefit deer, elk, moose and other wildlife.

Canada has no equivalent of Pittman-Roberts, although most provinces attach a conservation surcharge to hunting license fees. Alberta, for example, collects "Bucks for Wildlife" from hunting and angling licenses and uses the money to protect habitat. Conservationists in both the U.S. and Canada have recently proposed taxes on a wider range of wildlife-related gear—binoculars, telephoto, camera lenses and hiking supplies—so that non-hunters, too, can financially support wildlife conservation. "Teaming With Wildlife," if approved by politicians, will inject hundreds of millions of new dollars into wildlife agency budgets.

Overleaf: A bull elk stands in Canada's Rocky Mountains

than elk, but elk were often easier to hunt. Both on the plains and in the desert mountains of the Southwest, hunters sometimes dug pits in game trails and then chased elk herds across them. One historian wrote that the Apaches hunted deer by sneaking up on them disguised as other deer, but did not need such elaborate measures for elk which they considered "...not as smart as deer and . . . easier to get."

Modern human hunters prefer healthy, large deer and elk. They deliberately avoid killing sick or undersized animals. In this way, modern hunting has a different ecolog-ical effect than predation by wolves and coyotes that often kill the weakest animals. Some native hunting techniques had effects more similar to wolf predation than modern human hunting. For example, Osborn Russell, a frontier trapper, described Crow Indians chasing herds of elk until the weaker animals lay down to avoid further effort. The Indians killed the prone animals with knives, leaving the healthier and stronger members of the herd to escape.

Aboriginal hunters chose different animals for different purposes. The Pawnee, Sioux, Oto and Kiowas hunted elk mostly in summer, selecting yearlings (whose meat was tender) or cows (whose hides are most workable shortly after giving birth). In winter, Indians often preferred bulls because the larger animals produce more meat. On the other hand, winter bull elk have little fat left after rutting. Fat is vital for winter human survival, so pregnant cow bison was the food of choice for most plains tribes.

Because of their migratory lifestyles, mule deer and elk were only seasonally important. White-tailed deer, on the other hand, probably faced year-round hunting pressure since they remain at low elevations through all seasons.

Poachers Beware

Statue of bronze elk at Rocky Mountain Elk Foundation National Headquarters, Missoula, Montana

In 1995, a poacher used a crossbow to kill a large bull elk in Estes Park, Colorado. The old bull -- nicknamed Samson by local residents whose lawns he often grazed -- died simply because of his antlers. Outraged residents lobbied the Colorado legislature for harsher poaching laws and raised more than $55,000 USD to pay for a bronze statue to commemorate Samson's memory. Sculptor Carol Cunningham used photographs of Samson to create a model of the old bull bugling. "The statue will serve as a re-minder that poaching is not tolerated in Colorado," said Rick Spowart of the Colorado Division of Wildlife.

The new legislation, passed in 1998, adds a surcharge of up to $25,000 USD onto fines levied against poachers who kill trophy-sized animals.

Other high profile poaching cases involved a popular host of bowhunting videos who filmed himself killing elk in Yellowstone National Park, and a poaching ring west of Edmonton, Alberta, that slaughtered dozens of elk, deer and moose to sell their meat. Many state and provincial governments have followed Colorado's example by toughening their laws against poaching. Canada's National Parks regulations now provide for poachers convicted of killing trophy animals to pay fines as high as $125,000 CDN.

Why Parks Aren't Enough

Fences along the Trans-Canada Highway protect wildlife from heavy vehicle traffic in Banff National Park

National, state and provincial parks protect elk and deer from hunting and habitat loss. Nevertheless, when it comes to conserving ungulates over the long term, most parks are designed to fail. For one thing, parks rarely are big enough to protect whole populations of ungulates or -- perhaps as importantly - their predators. Colorado's Rocky Mountain National Park, for example, has neither grizzlies nor wolves. Alberta's Elk Island National Park has no predators larger than a coyote.

Where elk winter in national parks -- for instance on Yellow-stone National Park's northern range -- too much protection from predators can doom them to overcrowding and stress. Elk have grazed some national park winter ranges so badly that aspens are dying back and exotic grasses and weeds have begun to replace nutritious native grasses. In New Mexico's Bandelier National Monument elk herds threaten archaeological sites because their heavy grazing contributes to soil erosion.

History, in any case, placed most western national parks in scenically beautiful high mountains with little useful winter range. Summer visitors, seeing herds of elk and deer feeding peacefully in subalpine meadows, logically assume that the parks are ideal havens for wildlife. But when winter snows fall, ungulates have to migrate to less scenic, lower elevation winter ranges, often outside the parks. There they encounter cattle ranches, recreational subdivisions and highways. Increasingly unwelcome, they also face increased risk of death from road-kill, poaching, stray dogs and malnutrition.

Park managers know that drawing a line around an island of scenery offers little real protection in a world where animals range widely. Recently, many parks have begun lighting forest fires, reintroducing predators such as the wolf, and working collaboratively with their neighbors to manage whole ecosystems, rather than focussing only on parklands. A modern park manager might spend less time worrying about poachers than trying to help neighboring ranchers solve their winter hay depredation problems with elk. Ecosystem-based management, as the new philosophy is known, treats parks as part of larger landscapes and wildlife populations as fluid entities that cross boundaries.

Parks play a vital role in preserving wild nature and helping people learn about ecosystems. In the long run, however, the only way park managers can hope to conserve wild ungulates and other animals is to spend as much time working outside park boundaries as inside.

Some eastern tribes considered deer "real" meat, compared with other prey. The Sioux, for instance, originated in eastern woodlands before moving west onto the Great Plains. Even after the bison became their dominant prey, the Sioux continued to call white-tailed deer "tahinca," or "real meat."

Most native tribes set fires for insect control, hunting, warfare and other purposes. Frequent fire meant that the prairies had far less white-tailed deer habitat during the frontier era than today. In the more humid east, however, where trees and shrubs grow more prolifically, native-caused fires provided white-tailed deer with productive patches of young, nutritious vegetation. Most early explorers described white-tailed deer and, in some areas, elk as incredibly abundant—no doubt partly due to the abundance of young vegetation in areas burned repeatedly by native inhabitants.

Frontier North America

European colonists, for the most part, saw North America as a boundless land of inexhaustible fertility and endless bounty. Conservation was virtually unheard-of before the 20th century. Few of the newcomers had any understanding of ecology. Native people, entire wildlife species, and much of the continent's productive potential were swept away before a relentless tide of settlement.

Elk and deer were free meat. As water routes, trails and wagon tracks penetrated into unsettled country, naive native ungulates quickly fell prey to the need of settlers for both meat and cash. Frontier settlers rarely ran short of building materials, fuel or food; money, however, was in scarce supply. Deer, elk, waterfowl, pigeons and other wildlife fell by the thousands to be shipped back to eastern towns and cities and sold for hard money.

Explorers and settlers spent most of their time in just the part of the landscape where they were most likely to encounter deer and elk. Elk congregated in the productive habitats along rivers; those same rivers were the most important highways into the west. Deer, too, abounded in river bottoms and thrived in the rich forests that pioneers cleared for farmland. When aspiring farmers settled the river floodplains and began to cut and store hay for their livestock, and to grow grain and vegetable crops in what had previously been wildlife habitat, they soon found another reason to slaughter the animals. Especially during severe winters when snow grew deep, elk and deer would set aside their fear of humans in order to plunder haystacks. The settlers, unable to afford the loss of vital forage supplies, responded by killing them.

During the westward expansion that lasted from the 1500s into the early 1900s communication was poor, education scarce, and government ineffective. There were no game management agencies, conservation groups or other organizations to monitor what was happening to wildlife populations and try to regulate human behavior. The prevalent attitude was "Take it; it's free." If one person didn't shoot a game animal,

Fragments of Prehistory

Evidence of aboriginal use of elk and deer comes from bones and antlers in archaeological sites that date back at least 12,000 years. Sites with ungulate remains extend from Yukon and Alaska to the southern Rockies. Elk bones and deer antlers appear in archaeological sites at Santa Fe, Chaco and the Four Corners region. Researchers have found tools made of elk antler at least 4,000 years old in Montana.

Archaeological remains show that deer and elk became important prey—and sources of raw material for digging tools, hide scrapers, fluting tools and even as points for fishing spears—

about 9,000 years ago. Mastodons, mammoths, giant bison and other large prey animals that had prevailed after the retreat of North America's big continental glaciers died out. Deer, pronghorns, smaller bison and other modern animals replaced them in aboriginal economies. The distinctive Clovis projectile points of the mammoth hunters gave way to smaller flint points that archaeologists associate with the use by aboriginal hunters of atlatls (throwing sticks). There is no question some hunters used atlatls to hunt elk; archaeologists in Ohio found a flint point wedged into an elk bone.

somebody else surely would—so what sense could it possibly make to leave wild creatures unshot?

Exploitation and Extinction

Elk vanished earliest—in the mid to late 1700s—from Georgia and the Carolinas, where they probably never were abundant to begin with. By 1850, this magnificent wild ungulate had been extirpated from New York, Indiana, Illinois, Arkansas, Louisiana, Kentucky and Ohio. As settlement spread westward, elk populations blinked out one by one. By 1876, when General Custer led his troops to disaster on the bluffs above Wyoming's Little Big Horn River, devastation had already befallen the last elk in Ontario, Virginia, Tennessee, West Virginia and Iowa. Barely 20 years later, elk had vanished from virtually every state east of the Rocky Mountains and were on the verge of vanishing from Manitoba, Saskatchewan, southern Arizona, and New Mexico.

Deer fared little better. The same tide of settlement and commerce that swept elk populations to extinction also destroyed white-tailed deer populations and accessible mule deer herds. Native Americans and frontiersmen both participated in the first wave of eradication—the hide trade that destroyed an estimated one-third to one-half of eastern North America's deer population between the late 1600s and early 1800s. Mule deer populations remained relatively safe until colonists spilled west across the prairies in the late 19th century. A growing network of railways brought floods of land speculators, miners, settlers and repeater rifles into once-remote mule deer country. Striving to make the west safe for white settlers, U.S. army troops often slaughtered deer, elk and bison to starve native tribes into submission.

Whitetail numbers may have increased slightly in the 1800s as farmers opened up the eastern forests. By the end of the century, however, they were in decline again, along with the western mule deer. Biologist Stanley Young estimated that North America's deer population bottomed out in the late 1800s and early 1900s. By 1908, naturalist Ernest Thompson Seton estimated the entire North American population of whitetails—which may have exceeded 40 million when Columbus first saw the continent—at barely half a million. Except in isolated pockets of remote habitat, white-tailed deer were virtually extinct east of the Mississippi River. Mule deer, killed ruthlessly on their wintering ranges to supply growing towns and settlements throughout the Rockies, bottomed out at the same time.

Ecological historians Richard and Thomas McCabe describe the late 19th and early 20th centuries as "...the period of greatest hunting pressure on wildlife ever."

The dawn of the 20th century was one of the darkest times in the history of conservation. Unregulated hunting, commercial sale of dead animals, and the wild abandon with which colonizing humans took over and occupied wildlife habitat, all combined to rob North America of its primeval wealth. Whooping cranes and trumpeter swans hovered on the brink of extinction. The vast herds of bison and flocks of passenger pigeons vanished forever. White-tailed deer were extinct in most eastern states, and mule deer and elk were reduced to a few pockets of survivors in British Columbia, Montana, Wyoming, Colorado and Washington.

Conservation Movement

The darkest hour, the song says, is just before dawn. Early in the twentieth century, hunter-conservationists, naturalists and visionary politicians pulled together to build a whole new approach to wildlife conservation, unique in the world.

The U.S. Congress, responding to nationwide outcry over the destruction of wildlife, passed the Lacey Act in 1900. It outlawed interstate commerce in dead wildlife, and effectively ended the market hunting era by cutting surviving wildlife populations off from distant markets for meat and hides. In 1910, Canada's Prime Minister Wilfrid Laurier established a Commission on Conservation to organize efforts to restore wildlife north of the 49th parallel.

Visionary politicians set aside great national parks like Yellowstone, Rocky Mountain, Banff and Jasper to protect the last elk and deer herds. Wildlife refuges began to reclaim winter ranges previously claimed by ranchers. As wildlife numbers increased in these protected areas, conservation groups and government agencies began to trap surplus animals and ship them back to places from which over-hunting had eradicated them.

New regulations—established at the urging of new conservation groups—ensured that hunters could only take as many prey each year as the rebuilding herds could spare. With elk and deer hunting restored in places where the animals had not been seen for years, many hunters—painfully aware of the consequences of unregulated slaughter—became passionately committed to conservation. They formed organizations that helped fund research studies, habitat protection and a wide range of other measures to make North America, again, a place of abundant wild deer and elk.

North America's unique approach to wildlife conservation—public ownership of wildlife and funding of wildlife management, supported by strong citizen conservation groups who work to conserve habitat on both private and public land—is the 20th century's enlightened response to the carnage of the 19th century. Wildlife biologist Valerius Geist calls it the world's most successful model for wildlife management. The near extinction of elk and white-tailed deer, and the decimation of mule deer herds, helped bring it about. The remarkable 20th-century recovery of wildlife populations is proof of its success.

Conservation in the 21st century, according to noted elk biologist Jack Ward Thomas, will involve coping

White-tailed deer

with the consequences of that success.

National Parks

Even while a small group of hunting's elite worked to eliminate the worst excesses among hunters, establish wildlife sanctuaries and put effective game laws in place, another social movement was underway. Visionary idealists such as John Muir, George Bird Grinnell, Enos Mills and, in Canada, Gordon Hewitt and James Harkin recognized that elk, deer and other wildlife—and the wild landscapes in which they live—have value beyond the merely recreational or utilitarian.

The concern of influential and erudite frontier adventurers led to one of the most unusual inventions of the 19th century—the national park. Yellowstone National Park, in a remote part of the western Rockies, became the world's first in 1873. Banff National Park—Canada's first—came

into being 12 years later. Most of the greatest national parks were established during the early 20th century's progressive era: Grand Canyon in 1908, Glacier in 1910, Jasper in 1911 and Rocky Mountain National Park in 1915.

National parks caught the public imagination partly because of widespread concern about devastated wildlife populations. In the early years of the 20th century, park rangers and wardens concentrated on protecting deer, elk and other popular kinds of wildlife. Poachers were unwelcome—but so were predators. Old files in some national parks contain memos chastising rangers and wardens for not killing enough wolves, bears and mountain lions.

Success, however, carried a big price. Wolves vanished from most national parks south of Jasper by the 1950s and even the elusive cougar became rare. Lacking predators, deer and elk became so abundant that they began to damage vegetation, especially on their wintering ranges. In response to overpopulation, large national parks such as Yellowstone and Banff resorted to annual slaughters of elk, but these ended in the 1960s because of opposition from park visitors. The idea of park officials killing animals they were sworn to protect was hard for people to stomach. Animals starving to death on overgrazed winter ranges seemed more natural—especially since few people were around in winter to witness it.

The shortage of predators was not the only problem for the parks. Shortage of fire played a role too. Under natural conditions, most wildlife ranges burn regularly. Beginning in the late 1800s and early 1900s, however, western settlers fought fires aggressively. Park wardens and rangers worked as hard to eliminate fires as they did to eradicate predators. It didn't seem to make much sense to let parks burn up.

Without fire, however, forests have gradually expanded and grown thicker, re-ducing the low shrubbery and grassland that grazing animals need. By the 1970s deer and elk herds in many parks faced a two-pronged dilemma— without predation their numbers had far outstripped the ability of their winter ranges to support them, and those winter ranges were shrinking for lack of fire to rejuvenate them.

Restoration

Since the early 1980s, national park authorities have shifted emphasis from protecting and stabilizing scenic environments to restoring the dynamic interplay of natural forces—such as fire, floods and predation—that created the beauty of these parks in the first place. Most parks have some kind of fire program that—under carefully prescribed conditions to ensure human safety—allows fire back into the landscape. Some parks move roads and trails to allow flooding to rework the rich ribbons of green along streams. In 1995, Yellowstone became the first park to import and release wolves in a successful effort to put predation back into the picture too.

Ecosystem restoration is a new challenge for national parks—part of the continually evolving social and ecological experiment that began with the 1872 establishment of Yellowstone. Some aspects of ecosystem restoration, however, aren't as popular as the earlier wildlife protection measures. Smokey Bear has done too good a job of teaching people to fear forest fires. Free-ranging predators strike fear into the hearts of many that live near parks and public lands. An important part of ecosystem restoration involves reeducating humans who have lost their connections to the dynamic processes that keep ungulate habitat healthy.

Private Land / Public Wildlife

Wild animals belong to everybody, but their habitat often belongs to private individuals. State and provincial wildlife agencies—responsible for maintaining healthy wildlife populations—have little say over what happens to the habitat those animals need.

The dilemma, however, cuts both ways. Ranchers and farmers who grow grain and hay to feed their livestock often feel less than happy about seeing elk and deer eating those crops. When hunters buy licenses from the government to hunt publicly-owned wildlife, and then want to hunt those animals on private land, the situation can be particularly galling. The rancher gets no money for the animals that ate his crops—and now he or she has to put up with hunters too.

It isn't an easy situation, but most conservationists agree that it beats the alternatives. In Europe, landowners

Fenced In

Early elk and deer protection efforts yielded some little-known dividends—like the common "Page wire" fence. Writing in his memoirs, the New York Zoological Society's egotistical first Director William Hornaday credits himself for a style of wire fencing that remains popular more than a century later. Hornaday commissioned J. Wallace Page of Adrian, Michigan to manufac-ture 60 inch woven wire fence for buffalo, and 88 inch for elk. "That wire fence, as developed by Mr. Page and the author in 1888 and 1889, made possible a series of magnificent wild western buffalo-range sanctuaries, owned by the federal government, and dedicated to the semi-wild breeding and safe keeping of half a dozen species of American big game."

Hunter Conservationists

George Bird Grinnell

Brooklyn-born George Bird Grinnell began hunting at the age of only 11 or 12, using a borrowed musket to shoot waterfowl along the Hudson River. In 1870, newly come of age, he ventured west to Wyoming to collect fossils. It was the first of many expeditions including one to the Yellowstone area that first awakened his fears that greed might doom the West's spectacular wildlife abundance. "It may not be out of order here," he wrote in his report on wildlife conditions, "to call your attention to the terrible destruction of large game, for their hides alone ... Buffaloes, elk, mule-deer and antelope are being slaughtered by thousands each year, without regard to age or sex, and at all seasons ... During the winter of 1874-75 not less than 3,000 elk were killed for their hides alone."

Later, as editor of Forest and Stream magazine, Grinnell promoted conservation, better enforcement of wildlife laws, and establishment of protected parks for wildlife. He is widely recognized as the father of Glacier National Park—set aside at Grinnell's urging in 1910. Grinnell was a co-founder of both the Audubon Society (1886) and Boone and Crockett Club (1887).

Theodore Roosevelt

Until about 1905, prevailing wisdom was that Americans had a manifest destiny to civilize and control the new continent. Most believed that this must inevitably lead to the eradication of large animals. A one-time Wyoming rancher, noted big game hunter and President of the United

Statue of Theodore Roosevelt

States, however, felt differently. He believed that intelligent and principled humans could restore wildlife populations and sustain their abundance, even while continuing to hunt and share their habitat. Originally a bit of a game hog himself, Roosevelt's mature reflections and discourse with wildlife advocates such as George Bird Grinnell led him to adopt, in 1910, a new doctrine for the management of America's wildlife resources—"conservation through wise use." Roosevelt felt that wildlife was renewable, so long as hunters took less than the yearly increase. He also believed that conservation depended on hunters and others adopting voluntary codes of restraint and fair play in their interactions with wild animals. With other early conservationists, Roosevelt established a new society to promote better wildlife laws, sportsmanlike conduct and responsible conservation: the Boone and Crockett

Hunter Conservationists

Club. During his two terms as-President, Theodore Roosevelt established many federal wildlife reserves and national forests, and shepherded wildlife conservation measures through the legislative and budget processes.

Olaus and Margaret Murie

The Muries moved from Alaska to Jackson Hole, Wyoming, in 1926. Olaus, already a well-known caribou biologist and a seasoned big game hunter, had been commissioned by the U.S. Biological Survey to conduct an in-depth study of elk biology. The Survey hoped to find out why so many elk were dying on winter ranges. The Muries, who already had one child, added two more to their family during the five years that they lived in the lee of the Grand Tetons. Olaus spent countless hours afield, observing and studying the 20,000 head Jackson Hole elk population. His studies solved the mystery of massive elk winter kills: necrotic stomatitis, a bacterial infection partly triggered by artificial feeding of grass hay. He produced a classic of biological literature—*The Elk of North America*, published in 1956 - and helped set the stage for better management of the last large wintering herds of elk in the Rocky Mountains. Margaret Murie documented their life among the elk in her own book, *Wapiti Wilderness*. The Muries were later instrumental in the successful campaign to protect America's largest wilderness sanctuary -- the Arctic National Wildlife Range.

Aldo Leopold

No book has ever approached the impact that Aldo Leopold's *A Sand County Almanac* has had on conservation and public understanding of ecology. A well-thumbed copy sits beside the desk of virtually every serious conservationist in North America. A passionate hunter of big game and upland birds, Leopold ranged widely among the mountains and canyons of the American West after moving from the Midwest to Arizona in 1909. He spent most of his life working for the U.S. Forest Service, and helped conceive and develop its Wilderness program, starting with a successful campaign to protect western New Mexico's Gila Wilderness. His 1933 textbook *Game Management* was the first to synthesize the lessons learned from the painful American experience in rebuilding depleted wildlife populations. After taking on a professorship at the University of Wisconsin, Leopold bought a small, degraded farm in the sand counties and began the slow process of nursing it back to ecological health. In 1948—the same year that Leopold died—Oxford University Press published a book he had assembled during those sand county years. Crafted out of Leopold's mature reflections on more than half a century of conservation work and wilderness advocacy, *A Sand County Almanac* was an old hunter's gift of love, logic and wisdom to future conservationists.

own any wild animals on their land. As a result, the public values wild animals far less than they would if they felt they had a share in them. Poaching carries far less social stigma in Europe than it does in North America.

Wildlife agencies try various ways to reconcile the conflict between public deer and elk and private property. Most western states pay compensation to ranchers who can show that deer or elk have damaged their crops. The compensation funds come from money raised through sale of hunting licenses. Successful Wyoming hunters hand coupons over to landowners who can cash them in, getting a financial reward both for protecting habitat and allowing hunter access.

Colorado's Wildlife Habitat Partnership program not only pays compensation but provides fencing to ranchers to protect stored hay from hungry deer and elk. The program's biologists will even arrange to develop alternative food sources on public land. In Alberta, farmers can get free fencing to protect their stored feed and are entitled to a free landowner's hunting permit, but cannot claim cash compensation for damages.

Still, few programs solve the problem of elk trampling crops that sprout in spring, the ongoing nuisance of competition between ungulates and domestic livestock, or the inconvenience of dealing with unwanted calls and visits from hopeful hunters each fall. Frustrated landowners have little incentive—other than their own stewardship ethics —to protect wildlife habitat.

Woodland caribou

Over the past two decades, some ranchers have begun charging hunters cash for the right to hunt on their land. This practice is still illegal in Canada, but widespread nonetheless. By charging for land access, ranchers and farmers can profit from wildlife. Still, paid hunting access has many critics, especially people who have studied wildlife conservation history. They argue that paid access indirectly turns wildlife into private property and creates commercial markets for dead animals—and they point out that the last time North America embraced commercial trade in wildlife we nearly lost our wild elk and deer populations. The cost of paid hunting is another thorny issue—at up to $10,000 USD for a hunt on private property, very few children get to hunt there. Without children learning to hunt, the hunter-conservationist eventually may cease to be.

Hunting

Humans have probably always hunted ungulates. Some anthropologists, in fact, suspect that human consciousness arose as a direct result of our need to hunt and gather food.

Cave drawings in France, petroglyphs on sandstone cliffs in the southwestern U.S. and stone arrowheads in archaeological sites around the world attest to the importance of the hunt in primitive cultures. One of the attractions that drew colonists from Europe to North America was the opportunity to hunt freely for food—in Europe only nobility and landed gentry could hunt. Frontier self-sufficiency meant growing vegetables for one's own family and shooting wild game for meat.

Venison or Vegetables?

Ted Kerasote, "Eco-Watch" editor for Sports Afield magazine, feels that eating ungulates killed close to home has less ecological impact and more social value than choosing a vegetarian diet based on industrial farming. In his book *Heart of Home*, Kerasote says, "An elk shot near a hunter's home in the Rocky Mountains incurs a cost to planet Earth of about 80,000 kilocalories. This includes the energy to produce the hunter's car, clothing, firearm, and to freeze the elk meat over a year. If the hunter chooses to replace the amount of calories he gets from 150 pounds of elk meat with rice and beans grown in California, the cost to planet Earth is nearly 500,000 kilocalories, which includes the energy costs of irrigation, farm equipment, and transportation of the food...(and should also factor in) the cost to wildlife -- songbirds, reptiles, and small mammals -- who are killed as a result of agribusiness."

Deer and elk behavior offers clear evidence of the long relationship between human predators and ungulate prey. White-tailed deer, in particular, act like animals that specialize in dodging human hunters. Remaining still while a wolf or cougar walks by at close range is a sure formula for short life. Humans, however, have a weak sense of smell and often overlook immobile objects. Whitetails commonly lay still or silently sneak around behind human hunters—tactics that have served them well during thousands of years of intense predation by aboriginal hunters, then by pioneer Europeans and more recently by licensed recreational hunters.

Hunting, at its best, remains a uniquely valuable cultural—and ecological—institution. Hunters must form close and abiding relationships with deer, elk and moose, and the habitats those

Unfair Advantage

Human hunters, at least until recently, were inferior predators. We lack sharp noses, acute hearing, piercing teeth, stamina and speed. Aboriginal hunters compensated for their physical failings by employing teamwork and intelligent strategy. They set snares on game trails, cooperated to drive deer and elk into traps, and even made decoys or dressed up in costumes to deceive their prey.

Humans, just like the animals we eat, have been shaped by natural selection. The same impulse to use cunning and technology to compensate for our physical weaknesses -- bred into us over thousands of years -- persists in modern hunters. That impulse, however -- thanks to modern technology -- can lead modern hunters into an unfair and exploitative relationship with their prey.

Modern hunting catalogues advertise chemical scents that help hunters smell like elk or deer. You can buy infrared night-viewing glasses, hearing aids that magnify the sounds of approaching deer, automated animal calls that sound like amorous cow moose or lost fawns, rifles accurate to ranges of more than half a mile, camouflage, walkie-talkies and satellite positioning systems.

Techno-hunters know more about their gear than about their prey or its habitat. Hunting with gadgets is less about forming a respectful and intelligent relationship with the animals and habitats that sustain us than it is about ensuring success at all costs. Ironically, the quest for trophy heads that score high in the Boone and Crockett Society's record book plays a strong role in creating the demand for more gadgets—even though the Boone and Crockett Society's founders were among the first to call for voluntary restraint and foregoing of unfair advantage.

Technological cheating isn't a new problem. More than half a century ago Aldo Leopold wrote that "...the gadgeteer...has draped the American outdoorsman with an infinity of contraptions, all offered as aids to self-reliance, hardihood, woodcraft or marksmanship, but too often functioning as substitutes for them."

Venison versus Beef

Healthy diets are low in saturated fats and cholesterol. It makes sense, then, to substitute venison from wild elk, deer or moose for fat-rich meats from domestic animals. Wild venison is leaner than domestic beef or pork—an 100 gram serving of elk or deer has only 110 calories and one to two grams of fat, compared to 272 calories and 18 grams of fat in the same amount of lean beef hamburger.

Vitamin levels are also far higher. Since the fat doesn't marble the meat, cooks easily trim it from the edges of most cuts. Some people claim that deer meat has a gamy taste, but since most of the flavor is concentrated in fat, trimming the meat solves the problem. Domestic livestock—including farm-raised deer and elk—are often treated with growth hormones, antibiotics and other chemicals, as well as absorbing traces of pesticides from their forage. Wild deer in agricultural areas can contain some of the same trace chemicals. For the most part, however, those who hunt and eat their own wild venison enjoy healthier meals than those who find their meat under cellophane in the supermarket -- not to mention the aerobic benefits of spending long days afield in pursuit of their prey.

Exotic Invaders

Cheatgrass

Star thistle

Weeds such as Russian knapweed, leafy spurge, musk thistle and cheatgrass choke many western wildlife ranges -- an insidious kind of damage invisible to people who don't recognize the difference between healthy vegetation and weeds. British Columbia range ecologist Don Gayton says that cheatgrass -- a fire-prone and mostly inedible foreign grass -- now blankets more than 40 million western acres. Knapweed -- a coarse flowering plant loved by honeybees and nothing else -- has taken over at least two million more. Around Missoula, Montana, and many other western towns, virtually no healthy native rangeland survives. It's all weeds.

Most exotic weeds originated in Europe or Asia. Their seeds arrived in North America mixed into shipments of grain or vegetable seeds, or in bedding for domestic livestock. Once here, they could out compete native plants because they arrived without the insects, fungi and diseases that control their populations back home. Weeds thrive best where humans disturb native vegetation. Forest roads - like infected knife wounds -- create ribbons of knapweed and thistle that spread these weeds far into forests.

Logging disturbs soil too, allowing weedy infections to spread even more. If ranchers allow their livestock to overgraze riparian areas, weeds usually increase. Spring floods then spread them downstream where they invade more wildlife ranges.

When elk or deer overcrowd their habitat, the trampling and overgrazing can also make it easy for weeds to spread. Some weeds - such as burdock and hound's tongue -- have seeds that stick to animal hair. Eventually the animals rub off the seeds -- sometimes miles from where they got them -- and the trampled, manure-rich rubbing area becomes a new weed infestation.

Wildlife experts consider weed invasion one of the most insidious threats facing western wildlife populations. "Nobody's quite caught on to how bad it is," says former Forest Service chief Jack Ward Thomas. "Of all the perils that we face in wildland natural resource management, exotic weeds is one of the most underestimated."

Colorado wildlife manager John Seidel says the roots of the weed problem go back almost a century. "We had millions and

Exotic Invaders

Roads provide exotic weeds a path to new areas

cals. Agriculture Canada and the U.S. Department of Agriculture continue to search for and test insects that attack weeds. Several kinds of flea beetle, weevil and moth, imported from Europe, have proven effective at controlling plants such as leafy spurge and St. John's Wort. Still, biological control is risky -- insects imported to control weeds can become problems in their own right if they change their habits in North America and begin to attack native plants instead. A weevil released in North Dakota to kill exotic thistles, for example, nearly wiped out several native species.

Weeds are here to stay. Tomorrow's wildlife habitat can never again be like yesterday's. Even so, good land management can reduce the damage. Many western ranchers have figured out how to manage cows and sheep so that the animals cause little damage to native vegetation -- weeds find it hard to invade healthy rangeland. The U.S. Forest Service has cut back its road building program drastically. Fewer new roads and more sensitive logging methods will reduce the spread of weeds into remote forested areas. Land use planning that keeps roads and subdivision from opening up the landscape also helps limit the spread of weeds -- where local governments are willing to adopt such measures. And many county and municipal agricultural agencies have become aggressive in detecting new weeds and attacking them with herbicides before they can spread.

millions of sheep and cattle on this range here for years and years at the turn of the century," he says. "We're still feeling the effects of that as far as our habitat and our stream banks. It was the grandfathers of today's ranchers...they just had countless head of sheep and cattle here."

Chemical herbicides can be effective at controlling the spread of weeds if county agricultural agents and private property owners react quickly. Once an aggressive weed like knapweed or cheatgrass is well established, however, it becomes almost impossible to control with chemi-

47

animals live in. Hunters must develop self-sufficiency in the wild. They must constantly make value judgments, adopt ethical standards, and live with the consequences of their actions. Hunters, perhaps more than many others, understand the meaning of their food—because they seek it, kill it, and prepare it themselves. Serious hunters develop a passionate bond to the places and prey that they hunt, often becoming powerful and persistent advocates for conservation and habitat protection. The hunting urge remains a powerful part of human ecology, and a potentially powerful force in shaping the human spirit, even though few of us need to hunt our own food anymore.

The fact that few modern hunters need to hunt, however, makes hunting increasingly controversial. Hunters comprised more than 30 percent of the North American population a century ago; now fewer than 10 percent of us hunt. Some argue that hunting's time is past. At the heart of the debate between hunters and anti-hunters is the fact that to hunt, a person must consciously choose to kill another living being. Those who oppose hunting often assume that hunters hunt in order to enjoy the act of killing something. In reality, few hunters relish the death of their prey, especially if there is pain involved. Many grow to dislike it so much that they eventually cease to hunt at all—but they continue to know themselves as hunters. Jose Ortega y Gasset, one of the first philosophers to reflect on hunting,

wrote: "One does not hunt in order to kill; on the contrary, one kills in order to have hunted."

Ultimately, of course, one cannot eat without something else dying—one of the central ironies and binding truths of ecology. Some argue that, in that case, we should eat only meat from domesticated livestock. Domesticated animals, however, are simply those from whom we have stolen the possibility of escape. Hunting one's own meat seems to many people a more honorable way to engage those who die so that we can live.

Hunters come to know themselves through the intensity of the hunt—the feeling of predawn cold on a windy mountainside, the suspense of following a whitetail buck's track through melting snow, the feeling of a favorite rifle or bow in hand, the smell of aspen leaves, spruce resin, elk

viscera, and new snow. Hunters become, however briefly and imperfectly, predators. As predators they become acutely involved with sounds, movements, scents, the direction of wind, the locations of cover and shelter - they find themselves inside nature as full participants, rather than outside of it as observers. Long after a hunter ceases to carry a gun into the field, he or she remains a hunter at heart.

Deer farming

Commercial markets for wild animals are back, and conservationists are sounding the alarms. Unlike market gunners and hide hunters who devastated wildlife herds in the 1800s, the modern version involves agriculture—the breeding of captive deer and elk behind eight-foot metal fences.

Game ranching began in the 1970s as a novelty. Many biologists even supported the

The Boone and Crockett Club

One December evening in 1887, the young Theodore Roosevelt invited ten people over for dinner at his home on New York's Madison Avenue. The elite group of wealthy and influential big game hunters included three Roosevelts, George Bird Grinnell, Archibald and E.P. Rogers, J. Coleman Drayton, Thomas Paton, James E. Jones, John J. Pierrepoint and Rutherford Stuyvesant. By evening's end they had agreed to establish a new organization that would promote hunting, exploration, fellowship, and conservation. The new Boone and Crockett Club – named after two famous frontiersmen - promised "...To

work for the preservation of the large game of this country, and, so far as possible, to further legislation for that purpose, and to assist in enforcing the existing laws." Roosevelt's influence and Grinnell's ideas were equally important in the birth and development of one of the continent's first and most influential conservation organizations. One of the Club's first campaigns was to expand Yellowstone National Park and offer its wildlife herds better protection from poachers -- something that might come as a surprise to those who associate Boone and Crockett primarily with trophy hunting.

idea, because they thought that ranchers could profit while keeping forested habitats uncultivated. Elk and deer, they thought, would not need the intensive hay production that domestic cattle and sheep demand.

As game ranching has spread across North America, however, most biologists and conservationists have come to view it as a scourge. Game ranches manage captive deer and elk as intensively as any other livestock. The fenced compounds eliminate any chance for wild deer and elk—

and their predators - to use habitat that would still be available to them if the land were producing conventional livestock. Captive ungulate herds have proven to be breeding grounds for frightening diseases such as tuberculosis, chronic wasting disease and brucellosis. Game farmers have crossbred elk with red deer, and red deer have escaped from game farms into the wild.

Perhaps the most succinct criticism of game farming came from Samson Beaver, the Chief of an Alberta Cree

band: "What the hell is game farming? Now they want to put animals on reservations?"

Of almost 100,000 ungulates held in captivity in Canadian deer farms in 1997 according to the Canadian Venison Council, 35,000 were elk and 10,500 were whitetails. Other species include European red deer, fallow deer, mule deer and reindeer. Organizations such as the American Deer Farmers Association and the Canadian Venison Council have established codes of practice and worked hard to eliminate some of the

Orion: The Hunters Institute

Jim Posewitz

Fit and compactly built, Jim Posewitz has piercing blue eyes that have looked over a lot of wild, windy country. Posewitz worked for 32 years as a biologist for Montana's Department of Fish, Wildlife and Parks. In his spare time he hunted elk and other wildlife in the wilderness high country of the Rocky Mountains.

By the time he retired in 1993, Posewitz had become painfully aware that hunting was under siege in North America's increasingly urbanized culture.

Growing concern for animal rights and the environment, and increasing distance from wild nature, make it difficult for many people to accept hunting as a legitimate human endeavor. There have always been hunters whose behavior and ethics are disgusting. Nevertheless, Posewitz knew that enlightened hunters originally founded the North American conservation movement and played a critical role in bringing animals such as elk and deer back to abundance. He didn't want to see the cultural value of hunting lost because of misunderstanding and legitimate concern over the well-being of wild animals.

So Jim Posewitz called up a few hunters whom he had come

to know and respect during his lifetime. Orion - The Hunters Institute was born.

The biggest single focus of Orion is to promote ethical and respectful hunting. Posewitz believes that the privilege of hunting carries with it a heavy burden of responsibility. His book *Beyond Fair Chase—The Ethic and Tradition of Hunting* has become compulsory reading for hunter training courses throughout the West.

Writing in *Beyond Fair Chase*, Posewitz concludes: "Cultivating a profound respect for wildlife and the land will affect how we behave as hunters, how we act as citizen conservationists, and how the public perceives us. That, in turn, will affect what happens to the land, and it is the land, as wild as we can sustain it, that both the hunter and the hunted need to survive."

Orion - The Hunters Institute
P.O. Box 5088
Helena, Montana 59604

disease and other problems that plagued so many game farms in the 1980s. Many game farmers take pride in their operations and sincerely care about the animals they raise—but all are part of a phenomenon Valerius Geist and others see as the most serious single threat to wildlife conservation since the market hunter.

The captive ungulate industry has yet to prove itself economically. Commercially grown elk and deer appear on some restaurant menus, but venison remains a specialty meat in a culture addicted to beef, pork and chicken. The market for antler velvet has passed its peak, especially with the late 1990s meltdown of Asian economies. Most profits come from sale of breeding stock, but high prices in that sector can only last as long as the industry is rapidly expanding.

A profitable new market for captive ungulate fanciers is "canned hunts"—collecting money from people who want to kill large-antlered animals without the bother of actually hunting.

Habitat Conservation

"The rapid proliferation and intrusion of second-home and recreational development, with attendant road construction into former wild areas, have eliminated much vital wildlife habitat. The town of Vail, Colorado, now a thriving ski resort...occupies the site of the former wintering grounds of what was, until a few years ago, one of the largest mule deer herds in Colorado. The stillness of northern cedar swamps and hillside thickets that formerly provided undisturbed winter refuges for deer...now is constantly shattered by the whining roar of snowmobiles."

Almost a quarter century has passed since James Tre-

Pay to Shoot

A prospective buyer can pick his trophy without even leaving home. The outfitter sends him a set of photographs of each available bull elk, complete with the estimated Boone and Crockett score - even though these elk, being captive, can never qualify for the record book. If the client likes what he sees, he can pay by credit card. At the local airport, the outfitter meets the client and whisks him off to a private ranch where pen-raised, custom-fed bull elk await death in a fenced enclosure. The client shoots his chosen victim, leaving the outfitter to take care of all the messy work. The limousine returns the client to the airport and, in due time, he can show off his trophy elk and pass himself off as a hunter. He has paid well for this privilege -- as much as $20,000 USD for the kill alone.

It's a tidy arrangement that saves the so-called hunter the inconvenience of scouting for his elk, getting up before dawn, climbing steep hills, enduring cold hands or accepting failure. He never has to go near the blood or even touch his kill. No skill or scruples required -- it's hunting without the hunt. In fact, to many these so-called "canned hunts" are exactly the opposite of hunting -- an obscene parody.

Canned hunts became available in parts of Montana, Colorado and Wyoming during the mid 1990s. Public outrage erupted in 1998 when a member of the Montana legislature announced his plan to fence off 160 acres near Whitefish, stock it with thirty captive bull elk, and sell the right to shoot them for between $5,000 and $20,000 USD a head. The proposal by Bob Spoklie and his son Grant resulted in Whitefish residents banding together to circulate a petition for a statewide ban on canned hunts.

Elk hunter Bob Love insists that this sort of commercial killing has nothing whatever in common with hunting. In a public letter Love said: "...this abhorrent treatment of animals is indefensible on any ground other than greed...he's willing to threaten the integrity of wild elk herds and jeopardize the tenuous tolerance of hunting by a non-hunting populace in order to line his own pockets. Those of us who honor wild elk and choose to hunt them ethically should publicly condemn elk farms and canned hunts..."

Spoklie, in an interview for the Missoulian newspaper, had a simple response to his critics: "The law's on our side. Property rights are on our side...and we'll do as we please on our own land. These people come with more money than you and I have ever seen. You think that as a private landowner I'm going to turn my nose up at that just because some people who live up the road think it's unethical?"

In 2000, Montana citizens finally voted to ban hunt farms.

fethen identified habitat damage from modern lifestyles as the newest, and most devastating threat to wild ungulates. Since the publication of his landmark history *An American Crusade for Wildlife* the human populations of Canada and the United States have grown by 25 percent. Elec-

tronic communications and the rise of the service industry have moved commerce out of cities to wherever people want to live. Increasingly, they want to live in scenic settings near wildlife.

Some of the fastest growing centers of human population are among the most important

for ungulate survival. The conditions that make ideal winter range for elk and deer are also ideal for humans - mild winters, proximity to productive high country, and abundant water. Canmore, an old coal mining town at the gateway to Banff National Park, skyrocketed from less than 3,000 peo-

Ranching for Wildlife

Some Colorado ranchers make more money from the wild animals on their ranches than they do from cows and sheep. John Seidel thinks that's a good thing.

Seidel coordinates Colorado's "Ranching for Wildlife" program. Beginning with six large ranches in 1985, the program has grown to include 25 ranches that collectively represent more than 1,600 square miles of wildlife habitat. Ranchers who sign up for the program commit to develop wildlife and habitat management plans for their ranches and to provide free access for selected public big game hunters -- mostly those who get drawn for special cow elk licenses. In exchange, the ranchers receive a guaranteed allocation of bull elk licenses that they can sell or give away to friends. Those guaranteed licenses also entitle them to hunt during a three-month season, longer than other hunters. A ranch hunting license can sell for up to $15,000 USD.

"One of the ranches is owned by a private foundation. They've got 170,000 acres," says John Seidel. "They have the entire ecosystem for elk and deer. They had an unlimited amount of money to develop it. They've completely eliminated cattle from the ranch except for 120 head of

cattle -- that's a pretty low stocking rate. They make over a million dollars a year in gross revenue off their elk. They spend probably $750,000 on habitat and maintaining the operation. You pay $10,000 and you have a chance to shoot about a 250 to 300-point [Boone and Crockett score] bull. They have international clients that come in there continuously."

Critics like Wyoming's Robert Haskins say that Ranching for Wildlife and similar programs in Utah, New Mexico and California are just another way of converting public wildlife into private profits, while dressing it up as a conservation program. They point out, for example, that ranchers enrolled in the program have less reason to tolerate predators even than those who sell only beef. Others, however, believe it may be part of the solution to an urgent problem: how can society protect wildlife habitat on private property when skyrocketing real estate values tempt ranchers to cash in on the development value of their ranches?

"The biggest benefit I've seen," says Seidel, "is the attitude in the minds of the people who own the property. They change their view from a cattle operation to an ecological/ecosystem ap-

proach. My favorite line was from a guy who says the antelope aren't a problem anymore. He can get $1,400 for an antelope—that's a lot of lambs to a sheep rancher. And he doesn't have to feed it, he doesn't have to dock it, he doesn't have to touch it.

"One ranch is owned by a Swedish industrialist and he paid for this guy to get his Masters degree in wildlife management and he manages the ranch now. That wildlife manager is in charge of the sheep manager and the cattle manager—almost unheard of. That's a new direction."

Seidel is no fan of wildlife privatization—he oversaw the captive elk ranching industry for the Colorado Division of Wildlife before his publicly stated concerns about elk ranching so angered the industry that they lobbied, successfully, to have game ranching moved to the more booster-ish Division of Agriculture. Seidel, however, sees Ranching for Wildlife as a middle-ground approach where public and private interests overlap. It rewards ranchers who protect and restore wildlife habitat, offers new hunting opportunities for at least some members of the public, and protects critical wildlife habitat from the cancerous spread of recreational subdivision.

ple to more than 10,000 in less than a decade. New subdivisions carpet critical winter range once used by elk, deer and bighorn sheep. One, ironically, is called Elk Run. The elk ran long ago.

"In western Colorado alone," says wildlife biologist Tom Beck, "there has been 30 percent population growth in the last eight years - 3.5 percent per year. I see no break in it...Most of my neighbors are in their eighties. A couple is in the nineties. Their kids don't live here anymore and don't really want the land.

So it's when they die that it's most likely to pass into the hands of developers. I can't compete with these guys because they can pay a whole lot more per acre."

Conservationists have organized to try to save wildlife habitat from development. In some parts of the West they've had some success too. Conservation advocate Jim Posewitz points out that hunting groups started early in Montana—buying up over 240 square miles from ranchers who were plagued by wintering elk. The former ranches became winter game refuges. "At the turn of the century," he says, "biologists estimated only 500 elk along the Rocky Mountain Front; today there are more than 11,000."

More recently, the Rocky Mountain Elk Foundation has protected over 100,000 acres in the western U.S. and Canada by buying development rights to the land. The Nature Conservancy—which bills itself "the real estate arm of the conservation movement"—has protected even more.

For every success story, however, there are too many tales of permanent loss. Tom Beck feels that conservation won't work if it's based only on purchasing threatened wildlife habitat. "We don't have that much money and there's too much land. I'd rather see the time and effort go into teaching people the importance of learning to co-exist with these species. I think a lot of it's easy to do. But you can't come in here on winter range and build an 18-hole golf course...

"I think acreages are not necessarily incompatible. The problem is the laws we have in this state allow anybody with 35 acres or more to build without a subdivision permit. You go less than 35 acres and you need a permit. So that's what gives us ranchettes...Because of these laws we don't get cluster housing where maybe we could take 200 acres and put all the people on 20 and have the 180 acres open space and usable by wildlife. Instead we sprawl them out there and have one house every three

acres or one every 35 acres. Those laws were probably well intentioned when they were passed in the early 1970s but they've proven to be very destructive of wildlife."

Rural subdivision has a domino effect. It fragments ungulate habitat, results in more pet dogs to chase and harass the deer and elk that remain, and puts pressure on nearby ranchers to sell out or subdivide their land too. Montana's Bitterroot valley, areas adjacent to Yellowstone and many parts of western Colorado have lost vast amounts of ungulate winter range to incremental development.

Private land conservancy and land use zoning are two ways of heading off further losses. Perhaps most important, individuals need to understand that humans have choices—but wildlife doesn't. Habitat loss is forever.

Conservation through Chemistry?

Conservation groups strongly oppose the growth of the game farming industry. They consider farming of once-wild elk and deer demeaning to a native animal, a potential source of disease and genetic damage, and a threat to wildlife habitat. If these concerns are valid—and so far the history of the industry clearly suggests they are—conservationists may find solace from an unexpected quarter.

In 1998, medical scientists released a new drug called Viagra. It has proven remarkably effective as a treatment for male impotence and loss of sex drive. Already Viagra has made inroads into some traditional oriental markets for aphrodisiacs derived from bear gall bladders, tiger penises and deer velvet. If the trend continues, Viagra may further undermine the already-shaky economics of game ranching. Those who believe North America's native ungulates should be wild and free hope so.

Right: Sonoran whitetail at Madera Canyon, Arizona

Elk (*Cervus elaphus*)

Elk nursery herd

The first elk probably originated in Asia. From there, they gradually spread both west into Europe and east into Siberia. As their descendants adapted to new habitats and became increasingly isolated into different populations, minor genetic differences began to appear.

Today, most biologists consider the red deer of England and Scotland -- at one extreme end of the area colonized by prehistoric elk -- and the North American elk, or wapiti—at the other extreme end—to be the same species. When elk farmers bring elk and red deer together, they have little difficulty breeding —a key test for determining if animals are the same species. However the European red deer is a smaller animal than our elk. Its tail is longer and has a stripe of color down the top, the bull's antlers are less dramatic, and the roar of a red deer stag during the breeding season is a far different sound than the squeal and grunt of a rutting bull elk.

The animal we now know as the North American elk, or wapiti, eventually became the most widely distributed member of the deer family in North America. Before European humans invaded the continent, elk ranged from the oak savannas of what is now California right across the continent to the rich deciduous forests of New York, New Jersey, Virginia and Ontario. Elk grazed where the U.S. White House stands today. Some no doubt made it

as far east as the Atlantic Ocean. Elk occupied the "sky island" mountain ranges of southern Arizona and New Mexico and probably ranged into northern Mexico. Herds of elk occupied all the isolated hill systems and river bottoms of the Great Plains. By the time white settlers started spilling across the continent, elk had already vanished naturally from Alaska and Yukon, but they still ranged into northern Alberta and British Columbia.

To the Brink & Back Again

Elk fared poorly when confronted with the agricultural ambitions, firearms and sheer greed of the immigrants who flooded across the North American continent from the late 1500s until the beginning of the 20th century. Elk are large animals and their meat is good. It didn't take long before the newcomers—many of whom had arrived from European countries where only nobility could hunt big game—became proficient at killing elk. The colonists believed that they could never exhaust the fertility and abundance of this new continent. It took the extinction of the passenger pigeon, Carolina parakeet, Eskimo curlew and—in state after state—elk and deer to teach them that they were mistaken.

Today, thanks both to careful management of elk herds that survived the frontier slaughter and to restocking of barren elk ranges, the American elk has returned to most of its original western range, as well as parts of Michigan, Pennsylvania, Kansas and other eastern and Midwestern States. Elk range over more habitat in British Columbia, Oregon, Washington and Colorado than they occupied in the early 1800s. Surviving herds of Roosevelt and Tule Elk have increased, as have the last remnants of the Manitoba elk that once ranged across Canada's aspen parkland regions.

Elk represent a miracle of evolutionary history. Their recovery in the 20th century, in its own way, represents a miracle of conservation history.

Native Americans and Elk

Elk have been important to Native Americans for at least 12,000 years. Elk remains have turned up in archaeological sites at Santa Fe, Chaco, and elsewhere in the Four Corners region. Farther north, archaeologists have found elk remains and tools made from elk antler in Montana, Alberta, and many other parts of the West.

Natives not only hunted elk, but they also managed their habitat—most notably with fire.

Given a choice, however, most aboriginal hunters preferred other prey. Plains Indians only hunted elk when other animals were scarce or in summer when elk hide was most workable. Eastern tribes hunted deer more commonly, while most western tribes preferred bison and sheep. Elk were too patchily distributed in the landscape and, when frightened, ran into timber rather than across open country like bison. Tribes that hunted elk used techniques as diverse as chasing their prey into deep snow, running them down during periods of heavy snowfall, snaring or ambushing them along trails, and driving them over cliffs or into corrals.

Western tribes preferred elk hide for many kinds of

Elk Facts

Length:
bulls: 200-275 cm. (6.5-9 ft.)
cows: 200-250 cm. (6.5-8 ft.)
Weight:
bulls: 315-500 kg. (700-1000 lb.)
cows: 250-300 kg. (500-600 lb.)
Description:
Reddish-brown in summer, with a dark brown head and neck and yellowish rump patch and tail. Calves are russet-colored with cream spots. In winter, cows are brownish-grey and bulls are a pale cream color. Elk antlers sweep back toward the tail, rather than extending forward like other deer. Elk have small ears, shaggy necks, a "floating" run and a tendency to raise their faces when running from danger.
Life Span:
Twenty years at best; less than ten years is more normal.
Reproduction:
First breed at a year old on good range; otherwise at two. Single calves are usual; twins are rare.
Food:
Grasses, shrubs and bark in winter; forbs, leaves and grasses in summer.
Distribution:
Forested regions of western North America from southern Alaska and northern B.C., south to New Mexico, Arizona and parts of California. Isolated populations, mostly reintroduced herds, live in deciduous forests and hill systems as far east as Ontario, Pennsylvania, Virginia and Arkansas.

clothing. The antlers were also uniquely useful for making some kinds of tools. Indians used elk hide for tepee covers, moccasins, ropes and ties, and shields. Although it was less warm than bison hide, less elegant than pronghorn and less tough than deer, elk was the most durable hide. As a result, native women used elk skin for items that would receive a lot of wear. The Blackfeet may have gotten their name in part from their moccasins made of

Not Real Food

Bison

Bison was real food to the tribes of the Blackfoot Confederacy. They closely tied their seasonal round to the migrations of the great bison herds that ranged the Saskatchewan and Missouri River country before the coming of the repeating rifle. Large numbers of elk also lived on the plains - both resident herds that occupied isolated hill systems and river breaks, and migrant herds that wintered on the windswept western plains. Like other Native American tribes, the Blackfeet valued elk hide for the strong leather they could make from it, but Blackfeet tradition dismisses the rest of the elk as not being real food.

The Cheyenne and Arapaho, farther south, apparently valued elk meat more highly.

Kinds of Elk

Some taxonomists believe that six subspecies of elk ranged across north America when European colonists first arrived on the Atlantic coast.

Two of those now are extinct. The eastern elk *(Cervus elaphus canadensis)* used to occupy deciduous hardwood forests from Ontario south to northern Florida. Merriam's elk *(C.e. merriami)* was native to southern Arizona and New Mexico. Where elk occupy those regions today, they are Rocky Mountain elk *(C.e. nelsoni)* descended from animals imported after uncontrolled market and subsistence hunting had eradicated the original subspecies.

Rocky Mountain elk—the most widespread and abundant subspecies—are familiar to modern tourists who flock to Rocky Mountain National Park, Grand Teton, Yellowstone, Banff and Jasper. Manitoba elk *(C.e. manitobensis)* once ranged from near Edmonton, Alberta east through Canada's aspen parkland country to western Ontario and Minnesota. Visitors to Canadaís Elk Island, Prince Albert and Riding Mountain national parks can see this subspecies today, but agriculture has displaced the Manitoba elk from most of its original range. A few still range into northern Minnesota.

Two Pacific coastal subspecies are also limited to only fragments of their original range. The tule elk *(C.e. nannodes)* is the smallest, only about 2/3 the size of Rocky Mountain elk. Tule elk originally occupied the lush river bottoms and rolling hills of western California and survive today in a few small patches of their original habitat. Roosevelt elk *(C.e. roosevelti)* live in the moist coastal mountains of British Columbia, Washington and Oregon. There they summer in the high mountain meadows and migrate down to winter in the shelter of old-growth forests along the region's narrow river valleys and coastal plains.

Those who mourn the loss of original subspecies may find solace in modern taxonomy, which says they never existed in the first place. Based on genetics, all the elk of North America as well as those found in northern Mongolia are a single subspecies of the red deer. In eastern Asia, where other distinct subspecies of red deer occupy valleys and lowlands, elk are strictly mountain animals.

elk hide finished by smoking it over a hardwood fire.

Elk Habitat

Elk like hilly country that offers them a variety of choices. At some seasons they may spend more time down along streams and rivers in the mosaics of forest and meadow typically found where spring floods rework the landscape regularly. Other seasons find them on south-facing hill slopes where the sun is warm and grass is abundant. They often favor ridge tops that allow them to escape danger in heavy forest and flee in any direction. Even where elk used to live out on the prairie, they were most abundant in isolated hill systems or along the breaks and coulees draining down to large prairie rivers. Depending on the season, the weather, what kinds of predators are in any given area, and what condition different types of vegetation are in, elk will adjust from one habitat to another. At any given time, however, elk need an appropriate combination of security and thermal cover, foraging areas, travel corridors, and water. They also have special needs from time to time for mineral licks, social gathering places and isolated places for giving birth to their calves.

Food

Foraging areas change from season to season. In winter, elk congregate where snow is shallow or small shrubs protrude above the snow. There they either scrape away the snow—creating characteristic feeding craters—to eat dried grasses, or browse on green

Black scars show where elk browsed aspen bark

A Sorry Fate

*"**During the early settlement** of this part of Iowa, they were of great value to the settlers...But as has been the case too often in the history of the noblest game animals of this continent, they were frequently most ruthlessly and improvidently destroyed. In the severer weather of winter they were often driven to seek shelter and food in the vicinity of the settlements. At such times the people, not satisfied with killing enough for their present need, mercilessly engaged in an exterminating butchery. Rendered bold by their extremity, the elk were easily dispatched with such implements as axes and corn-knives.*

For years they were so numerous that the settlers could kill them whenever they desired to, but several severe winters and indiscriminate slaughter soon greatly reduced their numbers, and now only a few linger where formerly thousands lived, and these are rapidly disappearing."

Joel Asaph Allen, 1871:
Notes on the Mammals of Iowa

Elk damage: overgrazing can kill young aspen

Dental Dilemma

"I wish to make special mention of elk as these animals are...rapidly disappearing, and never can increase, so long as an order known as the "Elk's Lodge" is paying a premium for their teeth. It is a fact that there have been hundreds of elk killed in Colorado and Wyoming for no other purpose than to secure their teeth to sell for the use of members of said lodge."

Annual report of John Woodard, Colorado Game Commissioner, 1904.

The Benevolent and Protective Order of Elks—a fraternal organization devoted to community service—was anything but benevolent and protective toward elk during the early 1900s. Members considered it a mark of distinction to own a watch fob made from two elk canine teeth mounted in gold. The millions of members were a lucrative market for tooth hunters who killed thousands of elk just for the teeth, which they could sell for $10 a pair. The market dried up in the 1920s when, under pressure from conservation groups, the BPOE officially banned the use of elk teeth.

young twigs and buds of willows, serviceberry and other shrubs.

At other seasons elk may forage on newly-greened slopes, the lush edges of wetlands, in marshes, or on the forb-rich openings between stands of timberline trees. Elk prefer small openings close to security habitat, because feeding elk are vulnerable to surprise attacks by predators.

Grass is most important to elk when it is green and young—in early spring and where heavy grazing pressure forces grass to resprout. Unlike cattle and bison, elk rely heavily on forbs—flowering plants that grow in amid the grasses. Leaves are important in the spring when they are newly green and again, very briefly, in the fall when poplars shed their yellow foliage.

Elk depend more on grazing than browsing, unlike deer and moose. However, especially in winter, young twigs and the buds of deciduous trees and shrubs can become important survival foods. The upper-elevation limit of elk winter-range is often marked by heavily scarred aspen trees. The scars mark healed wounds from late winter browsing.

Elk, Moose, Wapiti

Many of the people who colonized North America in the past three centuries originated in Europe. There they already knew an animal called the elk—the same creature North Americans know as the moose. The European version of our elk, on the other hand, is called a red deer. The confusion over names frustrates biologists trying to sort out the ecological history of North America; if a German settler wrote of seeing elk, he might just as easily have been speaking of moose as of our American elk.

To sort out the confusion, some biologists continue to promote the idea that we should call our American elk the wapiti. Wapiti is a Shawnee word that means "yellow rump." As a native North American word, there is a lot of merit in the idea of adopting it; however "elk" is so well established that it just won't go away. Ironically the only place where the term "wapiti" has really caught on is among European biologists who use it not only for North American elk but for related varieties in eastern Asia.

Elk

Since aspens have green material in their bark, elk scrape the bark off with their incisors to get essential minerals and vitamins during the starvation days of late winter and early spring.

Mineral licks

Trace minerals can make the difference between good health and illness. Many human ailments—goitres, anemia, and immune deficiencies among them—can result from too little iodine, iron or other minerals. Elk often cannot get the minerals they need from their food. Plants translocate some minerals out of the soil, but only if the soil is rich in those minerals to begin with.

Where trace minerals are scarce, mineral licks become important elements of the elk's living environment. Deep worn trails converge on springs and seepage areas that bring dissolved minerals to the surface. In Jasper National Park, elk join mountain goats and deer to eat chalky silt in glacial deposits exposed beside the Icefields Parkway by glaciers. Some geyser basins in Yellowstone are also rich in minerals that attract elk.

Most mineral licks contain sulfate salts. Rumen bacteria use these to build amino acids such as cysteine and methionine that contribute to the proteins found in hair and other growing parts of an elk. Digesting the bacteria, the elk get vital nutrients that their normal foods can't supply.

Given the chance, elk will use salt blocks left out by ranchers for their cattle herds. They also lick road salt off highways in winter—a habit that produces many roadkills.

By the mid-1970s, up to 200 elk were dying each year on the Trans-Canada Highway in Banff National Park. Park officials finally solved the problem by fencing several miles of highway with elk-proof fences.

Elk, deer, moose and other grazing animals use natural licks throughout the spring and summer. Use peaks in May and June when animals shed their winter coats and cows give birth. The need to replace lost nutrients results in a need for mineral supplements.

Security

Elk rely on broken ground, water, heavy timber and distance for security. Often, when disturbed by a predator, elk will stand and watch before fleeing to safety. If the terrain permits them to keep a safe distance between themselves and the predator, they may only flee a short distance or simply stand and watch.

This behavior partly depends on the predator. Elk rarely run very far from wolves, but studies show radio-collared elk will run more than a mile to escape human hunters. Humans, after all, can kill from a distance.

Heavily hunted elk usually retreat to heavily wooded places at least half a mile from the nearest road, especially on steep slopes or ridge tops with Douglas fir, pine or other evergreens. Oak scrub in the southern Rockies is valuable cover for hard-hunted elk herds. Secure habitat is vitally important for accessible elk herds subjected to open hunting seasons. This is one reason many management agencies

close roads and restrict vehicle use on elk ranges.

Cow elk give birth in May and June. During the brief week or two when their calves are weak they must find security from bears, coyotes and other predators. Solitude offers some security since a predator may not find a lone cow as readily as a group. Cows, consequently, wander off by themselves to give birth. Some move into rocky, broken terrain at high elevations. Others hole up on islands in rivers or lakes.

Rivers and lakes offer another kind of security for hunted elk. Elk surprised by a wolf or bear will often race into the nearest water body and wade out until the water is two or more feet deep. In deep water, long legged elk have an advantage over shorter predators. If they remain long enough the predator will usu-

Kissing Cousins

For all practical purposes, the world's Northern Hemisphere contains two species of closely related deer -- the European red deer and the American elk. Under natural conditions the two would never interbreed because oceans keep them apart. Humans, however, complicated the picture when we exported captive American elk to Europe and Asia, and imported European red deer onto North American game farms. In Colorado, captive red deer have escaped into the wilds and, probably, mated with elk. Biologists fear that the resulting hybrids may prove disease-prone and ecologically inferior to native elk.

Flames of Life

Old antlers on a recent burn

The great Yellowstone fires of 1988 were not the disaster portrayed by the media. They were a long overdue revitalization of the park's aging vegetation, and a godsend for Yellowstone's famous elk herds.

Fire opens up forests that would otherwise grow dense, shading out food plants. The ashes fertilize the soil with a pulse of phosphorus and organic material. Deep-rooted legumes and alders thrive in the openings that remain after the flames have passed, adding a further pulse of nitrogen to the soil because of the nitrogen-fixing bacteria that live in their roots. The vegetation responds with a surge of growth, yielding high-quality forage for elk and other wildlife.

Forest fire almost never consumes all the available timber. As time passes, surviving patches of old trees become intermixed with dense patches of young timber and openings full of grasses and browse. The result is a diverse mosaic that gives elk ideal habitat—shelter, foraging areas and security.

Prairie fires are no less important. Grass fires remove unpalatable thatch, release minerals to the soil, kill back encroaching forest, and stimulate protein-rich, sweet new growth. Elk and other grazing animals often congregate on recently burned grassland, especially early in spring since it greens up earlier than unburned. Many early European explorers commented on the degree to which Native Americans used fire to attract their prey.

Natives may also have used fire to reduce populations of troublesome insects such as ticks and mites that infect not only wild ungulates but humans too. Modern problems with ticks and mites may partly result from the lack of regular grass and brush fires.

During the last century, humans have stopped lighting fires and become all too good at putting them out. In most parts of the Rocky Mountain west two kinds of natural fire are now missing from elk country. Lightning strikes, especially in high-elevation forested areas, used to maintain a productive patchwork of old, middle aged, young and recently burned forests—ideal elk summer range. At lower elevations, lightning fires were less common. Native people, however, often set grass fires in spring and fall, helping to sustain productive elk winter ranges.

In wilderness areas or large parks, authorities increasingly recognize the important ecological role of fire. Some have instituted a "let-burn" policy for natural fires started by lightning. Others, recognizing that lightning fires aren't enough or that natural fires can no longer safely be allowed to burn, have begun lighting fires deliberately under carefully prescribed conditions.

Outside of parks, forest managers sometimes try to duplicate fire's effects by changing logging and cattle grazing practices. Logging, however, does not replace fire. Logging produces different vegetation patterns, removes far more organic material, and fails to release phosphorus and nitrogen into the soil. Worst of all, from the elk's perspective, logging usually results in new roads that bring both weeds and guns. Even so, enlightened logging practices can produce many of the habitat patterns that result from fire. If management agencies protect enough older growth and are quick to reclaim the logging roads, forestry operations can benefit elk by opening up new feeding areas.

Cattle grazing, when managed with elk objectives in mind, can also duplicate some of fire's benefits. Grazing removes old grass and triggers re-growth of nutritious young grass. Many of the most productive elk habitats in the west support seasonal cattle grazing too, because biologists and ranchers have found that moderately grazed grassland attracts elk to the new growth. Heavy grazing, however, eliminates the dead grasses that serve as ground fuels that carry fire in forested habitats. Since cows don't eat young trees and shrubs, it also encourages woody plants to invade open forests and grasslands. Some ranchers and land managers now rest forested areas from cattle grazing every three or four years and use fire to burn off encroaching shrubs and trees.

Elk commonly retreat into water and bunch up when threatened by wolves

ally give up and go in search of easier prey. This defensive strategy doesn't work so well in winter, however, because if an elk retreats onto ice wolves or coyotes can quickly pull it down.

Shelter

Elk eat poor quality forage, especially in winter. They can't afford to waste heat energy, so habitat that protects them from cold wind and rain is critical. Heavy coniferous timber is particularly valuable since it intercepts rain and snow and blocks wind. Roosevelt elk depend on old-growth cedar-hemlock forests in their deep snow winter ranges. Snow rarely gets as deep beneath the protective canopy of the old trees as it does in young forests or openings. Along the Rocky Mountain Front Range from Banff south to Colorado, severe spring storms with strong winds and drifting snow often hit elk herds just

Ground Squirrels

Columbian ground squirrel

Wintering elk concentrate wherever the grass is most nutritious. Ground squirrel colonies are consistently popular sites. Ground squirrels eat grass too, and their summer-long nibbling keeps grass green and growing long after other plants have gone dormant. After ground squirrels retire to their underground dens to hibernate the winter away, the grass continues to grow. The first frosts trap nutrients in the growing leaves and stems for the elk who arrive soon after the first snow falls. Where elk inhabit prairie dog country, prairie dog colonies are just as attractive.

Elk grazing benefits ground squirrels too. Most ground squirrels need good visibility to help them watch out for predators such as prairie falcons and coyotes, so they avoid tall grass.

Native fires

"...in past years the Indians occasionally set fire to the forests, and burned out great areas in order to let in the sunlight, grow grass and create good feeding-grounds -- and also hunting grounds -- for hoofed animals."

William Hornaday, 1908.
Campfires in the Canadian Rockies

Left: Elk with velvet antlers

Roads and Elk

According to biologist Luigi Morgantini, elk suffered when the Alberta government built a forestry trunk road through the foothills east of Banff in the 1940s and 1950s. Following the line of least resistance, road engineers built this high-quality road through grassy meadows that line the Red Deer, James and Clearwater rivers. Within a few years, most of the region's elk had abandoned these winter ranges and shifted several miles west to smaller meadows closer to the mountains. Hunters reported similar habitat losses farther south where the forestry trunk road sliced through the formerly game-rich riparian meadows along the Highwood and Oldman rivers. Growing up in western Alberta during the 1960s and 1970s, I never saw elk or their sign in the bunchgrass meadows along the trunk road, and often wondered why. Later, as a biologist, I discovered that elk actual preferred to winter in the same kind of meadows in Banff and Jasper national parks' roadless wilderness.

Warden Jim Haskins of the Colorado Division of Wildlife says roads almost always displace elk. When hunters flood National Forest road networks in his district, near Craig, elk vanish almost overnight.

"We have such good access on our public lands because it's all roaded. This area over the years has been written up in publications...It started with deer and now it's the elk because we've got the White River herd down south and the Bear's Ears herd up north, the two largest herds in

Another close call on Jasper's Yellowhead Highway, Alberta

the state. Hunters just flock here. The access is so good up in the national forest that it stirs the animals up and once these animals go, they go. And they end up on private land.

"We speculated several years ago that our early seasons were causing us problems. Archery starts the end of August, muzzleloader season kicks in two weeks later. We were seeing just major movements of elk, big herds of elk, down onto private property, shortly after the archery season began. It got to the point where five years ago muzzle loaders were telling us, 'There's no animals up here.'

"The archery hunters blamed it on domestic sheep, recreationists, wood cutting, whatever. But without doing any research you could see a clear correlation between opening of archery and those movements. Well they wouldn't buy off on it and our game commission wouldn't buy off on it. So George Barrett at the

time started doing some preliminary investigations on it and showed a clear correlation between start of archery and elk movements off the Flat Tops down here. First of all he put radio collars out and then followed those elk and he was getting movements clear off the forest from elk that had been on the forest all year long. The only place they were staying were areas that weren't roaded or that had severe terrain where the elk were secure.

"After we did that for two or three years, we restricted the entry into those units to about 50 percent of what we felt it had been. And all of a sudden the elk were staying up and not coming down."

Biologist John Seidel agrees: "All the studies show that the higher the densities of the roads in an area, the less it's used by wildlife."

when they are weakest. In these open landscapes, small pockets of Douglas fir, pine and other conifers can mean the difference between life and death.

On very cold winter days elk will often bed down on south exposures during mid day, taking advantage of direct sunlight to reduce energy loss while they digest their morning meals. In summer, aspen forest also protects elk from the elements.

Too much logging can be hard on elk that must contend with hard winters. Logging companies that don't consider elk may remove too much of the most valuable thermal habitat—old growth coniferous forest.

Road-riddled Wilds

Green areas on maps can be deceiving. Canada's dwindling wild country is riddled by cutlines and roads that serve the oil and gas industry and forestry firms. U.S. national forests have eight times more road miles than the entire interstate highway system -- almost half a million miles in all! Roadless wild country is almost extinct in many parts of the west.

In 1999, the U.S. Forest Service declared a moratorium on new roads in most national forests. Agriculture Secretary Dan Glickman, announcing the ban, said, "Because a road is one of the most indelible marks man can leave on the landscape, it is our responsibility to safeguard the often irreplaceable ecological values of our unroaded areas..."

Western Canada's provincial governments, however, have yet to acknowledge that responsibility -- one reason, some conservationists argue, that southeastern B.C.'s elk population dropped in the 1990s to well less than half its former abundance.

Elk Family Life

Calf elk usually weigh from ten to 20 kg. (22 to 45 pounds) when born in May. Elk calves are reddish brown with pale cream-colored spots along their necks and backs. Although they stand soon after

Ripping up Roads

Most of the unneeded roads that crisscross elk habitat result from past logging or mining. Knapweed and thistles grow along the edges. Four wheel drives, dirt bikes and other off-road vehicles play on them. And elk and deer, for the most part, avoid them.

Increasingly, land management and wildlife agencies are trying to right past wrongs by putting old roads back to bed. In Montana's Flathead National Forest, for example, locked gates block many logging roads. British Columbia and Alberta simply post signs. In Colorado and Wyoming, bulldozed berms block access onto old National Forest and Bureau of Land Management roads.

Unfortunately, some off-road vehicle users delight in defying road closures. They've used bolt cutters, winches and even dynamite to get through locked gates. Berms barely slow modern all-terrain vehicles down. Signs end up full of bullet holes.

Near Yellowstone National Park, at least one Forest Service manager decided to take the job of closing roads seriously. Alan Vandiver commissioned a local contractor, Doug Edgerton, to design an all-purpose road-closing machine. Edgerton fitted a ten-ton bulldozer -- nicknamed "Rambo Cat" - with specially designed ripping claws that lift compacted road surfaces and aerate the soil as they scarify the surface. He also attached a metal brush rake to the bulldozer's front blade. On the back, a hoe and adjustable blade help dig out buried stream channels, pull debris onto the road from the adjacent forest, and pile and mound old road beds.

Once Rambo Cat is finished with a forest road it looks like an earthquake hit it. Dead trees strewn across the surface block all-terrain vehicles and provide lots of shelter for grasses, shrubs and young trees that sprout in the newly-cultivated soil. The natural contours are restored. Streams flow freely where culverts or muddied crossings were before.

"I believe in habitat," Edgerton said in an interview for High Country News; "I believe in fewer roads." National forest lands in the Yellowstone ecosystem, thanks to his invention, now have at least 200 miles less road -- and more habitat.

National Elk Refuge

The National Elk Refuge.

The Jackson Hole country, along the base of Wyoming's Grand Tetons, once teemed with elk, bears, cranes and beavers. Early in the 19th century, mountain men found the valley's lush riparian wetlands and set to work mining the abundant beaver fur. By the 1850s the beavers were gone, and so were the trappers. But the Jackson Hole country was no longer unknown, and it was not long before white men returned.

Ranchers and Mormon settlers set down roots in Jackson Hole in the late 1880s. They broke ground for crops, irrigated hay meadows, and brought herds of cattle to stock the grassland ranges. No sooner had the newcomers gotten settled than they had to contend with elk--thousands of them.

Early settlers estimated that between 15,000 and 25,000 elk descended from the high mountains to winter in Jackson Hole during harsh winters. As settlement spread, the elk found increasingly less winter range. Their grassy parks and meadows grazed down by cattle or cut for hay, the elk quickly learned to forage on haystacks instead. Some ranchers adopted a live-and-let-live philosophy, but others resented watching their forage stores disappear by mid winter. The carcasses of starved elk littered the range during particularly severe winters in the 1890s and early 1900s.

D.C. Nowlin, Wyoming's State Game Warden, felt the interests of ranchers and elk alike would best be served by segregating the elk and feeding them in severe weather. In 1910 the plight of the valley's starving elk became so alarming that the state legislature arranged to buy all the available hay in the area to feed the animals. The next winter, however, was even worse: more than 2,000 elk died and almost all the herd's calves.

On August 10, 1912, the U.S. Congress finally approved funds to buy land for elk, and the National Elk Refuge was born. The refuge has grown from a mere 4 ´ square miles in 1916 to more than 37 square miles today.

The small size of the original refuge, and the large size of the elk population, meant that management of the elk refuge during its early years largely consisted of feeding hay to wintering elk herds. Since the animals were safe from hunters while on the

Jackson Hole, Wyoming

From 5,000 to 15,000 elk winter each year on the lush meadows of Wyoming's National Elk Refuge.

refuge and food was guaranteed, the effect of the refuge was to bring elk out of the mountains earlier each year and send them back later. By concentrating elk in the area longer and longer each year, the refuge actually increased the headaches of neighboring ranchers.

The National Elk Refuge reopened to controlled hunting in 1943 because the elk were becoming so conditioned to easy living that many simply stayed on the refuge all year round, consuming forage in summer that managers wanted to save for winter feed. Seven years later, when the U.S. Congress established nearby Grand Teton National Park, hunting became a controversial issue again. Local ranchers and hunters worried that too much protection would

let elk numbers increase to more than the limited winter range could support. Grand Teton remains one of the few parks in North America where licensed hunters still hunt elk.

The elk that congregate on the neighboring refuge's feedgrounds, however, often become diseased because of the unnatural crowding they endure while in a weakened state. Feedgrounds - - like game farms -- are ideal breeding grounds for disease. One survey found that 37 percent of elk on feedgrounds had brucellosis, compared to less than 2 percent of elk wintering on natural range. That may change soon; in the winter of 1998/99 wolves from nearby Yellowstone National Park found the refuge and began to kill sick animals.

National Elk Refuge staff try to

minimize artificial feeding of elk. Some winters, elk never see a feed line. Instead, they forage on irrigated hay, recently-burned native grasslands, and other natural forages. During cold, snowy winters, however, refuge staff still spread long lines of alfalfa pellet feed across the feeding grounds. Hardy winter tourists can sign up for hayrides that offer a closeup view of more elk than most people see in a lifetime.

In spring, local Boy Scouts descend on the refuge to collect thousands of pounds of cast antlers that they auction off in Jackson Hole in one of the most unique fund-raising events anywhere.

Overleaf: Bull elk during the autumn rut

birth and can follow their mothers within hours, they lack the muscles and stamina to flee from predators. Instead, when danger threatens, a young calf responds by stretching its neck flat on the ground and lying perfectly still. Hunting bears, wolves, coyotes and other predators may scent the motionless animal if they pass near enough, but its camouflage coloration and utter lack of movement ensure that predators who rely on their eyes won't find it.

Newborn calves grow rapidly, more than doubling in size within two weeks of birth. During those critical early weeks, calves spend most of their time in hiding. They get up only to nurse and follow their mothers for brief periods. A nursing calf bunts its mother's udder several times with its face to get the milk flowing, a behavior that looks annoying to a watching human. The nursing cow takes it as a matter of course. Mother elk rarely travel far, spending a great deal of time feeding on the succulent green vegetation that is at its peak by early June.

After three weeks, calves become more active and their mothers commonly band with other cow elk into small cow-calf herds. The calves frequently play together, chasing one another, jumping, kicking and turning in circles. Young elk seem to take special delight in racing through shallow water. Although calf elk already graze on vegetation by early summer, they continue to suckle their mothers well into the fall. Some biologists report seeing large calves still nursing occasionally in late winter, but most stop nursing about six months after their birth.

Elk Social Life

Among North America's wild deer, only caribou are more gregarious than elk. Outside the breeding season, bull elk commonly associate in small "bachelor herds" which only break down in August when the bulls separate to join cow-calf herds. Soon after the end of the rut, bulls forget their recent antagonism and join up with one another again.

Summer herds of cows and calves are usually small. In most forested ranges, they may contain from three to 10 cow-calf pairs. In open country where elk numbers are high, on the other hand, a nursery herd may have up to 100 females.

An elk herd looks more stable than it is. Individual elk and family units move from one herd to another fre- quently. To the casual observer, the herd remains the same from week to week, but in reality there may be many different elk in the herd each time. Biologist John Woods radio-collared more than 40 different elk in one Banff National Park study. He found that some traveled frequently from one mountain valley to another, turning up in one herd one day and an entirely different herd a couple days later.

As summer days grow shorter, elk react by producing different concentrations of hormones. The cows begin to come into heat late in August or early in September. Bulls, attracted to cow-calf herds by the changing scent of the adult cows, become aggressive. Dominant older bulls harass adult cows and prevent their escape, gathering them into harems of up to 20 or more cows. The rut changes the ba-

Beavers

Beavers and elk share a common taste for willows and aspen. Where elk become too abundant for lack of predators— as happened in Rocky Mountain, Yellowstone, and Banff national parks during the late 20th century—beavers come out the losers. Wintering elk concentrate in riparian areas and browse young trees and shrubs so heavily that, eventually, stands of aspen and willow simply die out.

Starved of their food supply, beavers have no choice but to move on. Without beavers to dam up small streams, the water table drops and riparian meadows become too dry to support trees and shrubs.

Beavers help to maintain elk habitat

Where wolves and other predators keep elk numbers in check, beavers and elk make a good combination. Beaver dams create wetland habitats that elk thrive in.

sic herd unit from cow-calf nursery herd into breeding harem.

After the rut, the cows, calves and young bulls remain together, often joining with other herds until, by early winter, great wintering congregations of from 500 to well more than 1,000 elk may gather on winter ranges. Many elk herds are migratory, moving with the first snows from high-elevation summer ranges to wintering areas to avoid deep snow.

Rutting Season

When September's brief golden glory sweeps across the aspen forests of the Rocky Mountains, the frosty air shivers to the sound of bugling elk. Rutting season, when

hormone-charged bull elk gather harems of cows and defend them from other hopefuls, peaks in the last week of September and the first two weeks of October in Colorado and New Mexico. In the Canadian Rockies, elk rut two or three weeks earlier.

Cow elk come into estrous—a state when they are ready to mate—only for a few short days. A single dominant bull elk may breed up to 10 or 20 cows during the rut as each in turn comes into estrous. Any cow that fails to breed will come into estrous again about a month later and, if again she fails to become pregnant, a month after that.

Because bulls are both vocal and fiercely competitive in

the breeding season, many hunters prefer to hunt bull elk during the rut. Hunters use elk bugles and whistles to mimic the bugling of amorous bulls. Small diaphragm calls carried in a hunter's mouth can also mimic the sounds of cow elk or calves. An accomplished elk caller can persuade a nearby bull to sneak in close in hopes of stealing cows from another bull.

Some wildlife biologists, however, argue that hunting during the rut is bad for elk populations. When a hunter kills a dominant herd bull—especially if heavy hunting already has created a shortage of breeding-age males—he can disrupt the rut enough that some cows finish their first es-

Safety in Numbers

Elk seek safety in the herd

When Yellowstone's Soda Butte wolf pack found its way south to the National Elk Refuge early in 1999 observers watched as the wolves tried to penetrate tightly-massed herds of several hundred elk. As long as the elk remained tightly clustered, the wolves were stymied.

Large herds may result partly from elk having to congregate on small parts of the winter landscape. Herding, however, is also a defense mechanism against predation by wolves and other predators. A herd is collectively more alert than an individual. Predators that zero in on solitary

animals may have more difficulty attacking a herd or selecting a target from among many elk. Sick or weak animals unable to keep up with the herd are quickly singled out by predators. Their deaths buy safety for their healthier herd mates -- as well as reducing competition for limited winter forage supplies.

Life in the open seems to stimulate formation of large herds. Both elk and deer form their largest herds when deep snow forces them into open country, out of the sheltering safety of forests. Similarly, woodland and mountain caribou -- which live almost entirely in forests -- rarely form large herds even though the closely related barren-ground caribou of the open arctic tundra commonly mass in the tens of thousands.

During the rut, a breeding harem may include up to 20 or more cows.

trous period unbred. Even if another bull breeds a cow during her next estrous, her calf will be born several weeks late and, inevitably, go into the following winter undersized. Predators and hard winters usually kill late calves because of their small size.

Where elk are abundant, human access limited, and hunters scarce, hunting rutting bulls causes little harm. Many national, state and provincial forests, however, have many roads and hordes of hunters. Colorado limits hunting during the elk rut only to archery hunters who are normally less efficient at killing elk than hunters who use firearms. British Columbia and Alberta have open general seasons during the rut.

National parks and other protected areas normally prohibit or restrict the use of elk bugles to call elk during the rut. Park officials worry that too many enthusiastic buglers may stress or exhaust dominant bulls.

Communication

Elk are the most conspicuously vocal of North American deer, but the dramatic bugling of the fall rutting season is only one specialized form of communication. Elk bugle to show their dominance and warn off other bulls. Cow and calf elk are no less vocal, yelping and barking to keep in touch with one another in heavy cover, and to express alarm or aggression.

Elk are strong-smelling creatures, as any serious elk hunter knows. During the rut, bull elk urinate on their hind legs to strengthen the already-pungent odor of secretions from the tarsal glands on their hind legs. Getting into the spirit of things, some bulls often urinate repeatedly in muddy soil and then wallow in it, caking themselves with rank-smelling mud. A freshly-mudded bull elk stalking feverishly about in the height of his mating frenzy is a truly horrifying sight—but not, apparently, to females of his own kind.

Besides vocalizations and odors, elk communicate by body language. Dominant cow elk rush-charge lower ranking members of the herd and strike out at them with their forelegs. A subtle change in body position—turning sideways or tilting the ears out and forward—can signal dominance or aggression. Likewise, an elk that lowers its head and lays its ears back shows other elk that it wants to avoid conflict.

Not all communication is serious business. Calf elk, yearlings and—sometimes—adults play spontaneously, chasing one another in circles, splashing through shallow water, or playing king of the castle. I once watched four sleek young bulls trotting about af-

Elk foraging in the snow

ter a May rainstorm, frequently rising on their hind legs and pirouetting or bucking before thundering off in mock pursuit of one another—evidently for the sheer joy of being alive. Play behavior is most common when food is abundant and nutritious, perhaps because elk have energy to spare and feel invigorated.

Elk Through the Seasons

Elk lose weight all winter until the first greenery begins to appear in April. As the snow pack melts, elk herds break into small groups and disperse into the greening landscape. Cows give birth in late spring, just in time for the most bounteous time of the year when vegetation is most green and nutritious. This is also when the bulls—still solitary or in small bachelor groups—put on their fastest antler growth.

Bull elk fatten throughout the spring and summer while their horns are growing, reaching their peak body weights in early September when the annual rut begins. The intense activity that consumes bull elk during the month-long rut, however, consumes most of their body fat and leaves them in generally poor condition for winter. Cow elk, on the other hand, put much less energy into the rutting season. They can continue to gain weight until late November.

Elk are typically a burnished red-brown color in summer, cows and bulls alike. As the heavier winter coat grows out, however, it becomes easy to tell adult bulls from cows even at a considerable distance, simply from

Yellow Snow

How do you know if wintering elk are dining well?

Look in the snow.

Researchers at Montana State University have worked out a technique for analyzing urine-soaked snow patches to check on the nutritional status of elk. The scientists measure the ratio of urea nitrogen to creatinine -- a protein -- as well as the ratio of creatinine to another protein, allantoin. As elk begin to starve or grow unhealthy, those ratios change. Results so far suggest that biologists may be able to tell healthy winter elk from nutritionally-deprived ones this way. Where wildlife managers try different techniques to improve habitat, yellow snow might help them find out what works best.

Elk drag their feet even in shallow snow.

their color. Bull elk are a pale tawny or cream with a dark brown neck and head. The contrast between body and neck is less pronounced in females, because their body color is a darker brown. The difference is particularly evident as winter progresses, so bulls are recognizable at a distance even after they shed their antlers in mid winter.

Once breeding is over, bull elk really contribute little to the population. Pregnant cows, on the other hand, carry the future of the herd in their uteruses. Abundant fat and good condition are important to cows. If a few bulls starve or fall victim to predators, that is of far less consequence to the herd. This may account for the fact that bull elk often winter in heavier forest and at higher elevations than cow-calf herds. Their larger size helps them travel in deep snow and dig for forage. By wintering in marginal habitat, they do not compete for limited food with pregnant cows. Some ecologists speculate that this behavior may have been selected for through thousands of winters since it increases the likelihood of the herd surviving even if individual bulls do not.

Lone bulls in deep snow are vulnerable to predators such as wolves, but the fact that predators usually hunt the more accessible parts of the landscape partly offsets that vulnerability. Bulls are more easily caught, but less frequently found.

Winter

Deep snow is unkind to elk. Unlike moose, which have long legs and a remarkable high-stepping gait—or caribou whose small bodies and large feet help keep them from sinking into deep snow - elk are poorly designed for winter travel. Elk have heavy bodies, small feet, and an energy-wasting style of walking which forces them to drag their feet through the snow once it reaches more than a foot in depth.

This, no doubt, is why elk are rare in Canada's boreal forests. Nonetheless, western elk have found ways to compensate for the fact that winter renders much of the mountain landscape inhospitable to them. The key to survival for many elk populations is migration. As winter snows begin to accumulate on their high summer ranges, elk travel to winter ranges as much as 50 miles distant.

Even at low elevations, snow sometimes gets deep. Early ranchers, fooled by a few open winters when winds swept the western ranges bare, learned this to their dismay. Free-ranging cattle died by the thousands during hard winters like those of 1886, 1887, and 1906. Domestic cattle originated in southeastern Asia where they never had to evolve responses to snow cover.

Elk are at greatest risk for disease in captivity or at feeding grounds.

Diseases and Parasites

Elk are great habitat for a lot of other animals that need easy food, comfortable temperatures, and free transportation. Their large bodies have lots of places for worms, flukes, fly larvae and other creatures to make themselves comfortable. Biologists have identified at least 28 different parasites that make their homes on or in elk. Healthy elk rarely have much difficulty sharing with ticks, worms and fly larvae. Under some circumstances, however, parasites can become so abundant that elk sicken and either die or become vulnerable to disease. Diseased or parasite-ridden elk are easy pickings for predators such as wolves, coyotes and bears. Where predators are scarce, however, weakened elk linger on and often spread the parasites and diseases to others.

When elk become crowded in game farms or on winter feeding grounds, their close contact and reduced vigor improves the prospects for parasites. Not only can the parasites travel more easily from one elk to the next, but the weakened bodies of their hosts are less able to fight off the parasites. Elk forced to live on over-grazed ranges or in damp conditions can also be vulnerable.

Some parasites may be more common now than they used to be. Prairie and forest fires were once more common. Fire no doubt helped keep tick, snail and other invertebrate populations at low levels. Transplanting elk from one area to another helps spread diseases and parasites

Many, consequently, starved to death simply because they didn't know that good grass was only a few inches from their noses.

Unlike cattle, however, elk instinctively paw away the snow to find grass, creating distinctive feeding craters that pockmark snow-covered slopes. They almost always travel into the wind, while cattle turn their backs to blizzards and drift into snow-filled coulees or bunch up against fences.

Hard winters taught early cattle ranchers to put up sup-plies of winter feed for their ill-adapted livestock—setting the stage for future conflict once elk learned to raid haystacks.

Even though elk can dig through snow for food they often die in late winter anyway, especially when crowded onto over-grazed winter ranges during extended snowy periods. Winter, for most elk herds, is a season of slow starvation. Elk conserve their energy by resting in sunny spots during the day and foraging wherever they can find grass and browse with the least effort.

Urban Elk

Even urban elk are wild animals

Banff National Park wardens have a problem. A booming tourist town sits right in the middle of the park's main elk range. Elk long ago discovered Banff townsite's fertilized lawns and tasty garden ornamentals. When wolf packs returned to the Bow River valley in the late 1970s, elk found another reason to hang around the town -- wolves rarely go there.

By the late 1990s most of the valley's elk considered the townsite home. Exposed to constant contact with people -- more than five million people visit Banff each year -- the elk first lost their fear of people, and then started getting annoyed with them. Tourists constantly crowded feeding elk, hoping for good photos. Curious onlookers riled bugling bulls during the fall rut. Cow elk gave birth in backyards and then had to deal with "oh-isn't-it-cute" attention.

As the town's elk population grew, the once-placid animals began attacking people. At first wardens responded by trying to haze the elk away or move people back. Unfortunately, with up to 500 elk and thousands of people using the town at any given time, crowd management didn't work. Next, they tried sawing antlers off the most aggressive bulls and tranquilizing some of the more chronic offenders before hauling them off into the wilds.

That didn't work either. The attraction of high quality forage and safety from predators made the town too attractive, and the sheer number of tourists made aggressive encounters inevitable. Some elk even began attacking people who did everything right -- avoiding eye contact and giving the animals a wide berth. When elk attacked more than 60 people in 1998 -- including schoolchildren and town councilors -- Parks

Canada created a task force to deal with the problem.

Feelings run high when people feel vulnerable -- and a confrontation with a 500 pound elk is a sure recipe for vulnerability. After an elk trampled his preschool son, one Banff resident said, "Elk no longer fear man as a predator. We have to push them out and keep them out."

Attacks can result from cow elk defending their newborn calves or, in fall, from agitated bull elk. Some individual elk, after frequent encounters with humans, simply become cantankerous. A pedestrian who tries to walk past an aggressive elk might suddenly find him or herself facing a towering animal with flailing hooves. Others have been injured when elk harassed by photographers stampeded through watching bystanders or across crowded schoolyards.

Local residents have another

Urban Elk

A young bull elk signals aggression with his ears

golf course and keep people out in winter in hopes that wolves will begin to hunt elk closer to the town. The elk task force felt that a dark, quiet golf course might be more attractive to wolves.

They might have been right. By the spring of 2001, wolves and cougars were regularly hunting elk and deer right inside the boundaries of town. Even so, elk continue to use the town as a refuge and likely will, until the town in fenced.

Urban elk are a problem not only in Banff, but also in Jasper, Gardiner, Estes Park and other resort towns that occupy elk habitat in or near protected areas. After elk attacked 626 people in a period of 15 years -- seriously injuring 38 -- Jasper National Park officials bit the bullet in 1999 and started trucking elk out of town. Park wardens moved close to 200 elk to distant locations in hopes of getting the most habituated animals far from the nearest lawn. Ironically, some of those elk promptly moved into the town of Slave Lake, Alberta and began bullying local residents there.

Trapping aggressive elk or culling the herds, however, is only a short term fix. It doesn't deal with the real problem. Moving the towns would make more sense: people can make resorts anywhere but elk have considerably fewer choices. People, however, don't like to step aside for nature. A more ecologically-based solution might be to ban edible landscaping from towns and use trained dogs to harass urban elk so that they no longer associate towns with safety from predators.

reason for concern about the growing urban elk herd. They eat everything in sight. Former mayor Leslie Taylor laughs ironically when she looks at her garden. Trees and shrubs are pruned back and her flowerbeds cower behind custom-made metal screens. "We tried wire fencing but the elk just broke it down," she says.

A panel of experts completed an exhaustive study of the Banff Bow Valley in 1996 to find out how to restore the heavily-developed national park's ecological health. They recommended enclosing most of the town with fences to keep elk and bears out. Parks Canada revised the park's

management plan in response to their recommendations, but refused to consider fencing. In a subsequent meeting with the elk task force, park ecosystem manager Dave Dalman said, "Fencing, in terms of the townsite as a whole, is just not in the cards. Then people are living in a compound."

Instead, for starters, park wardens built a corral-style trap and captured more than 200 elk, including most of the worst offenders. They relocated the elk outside the park and began aggressively harassing those that remained. A local resort -- Banff Springs Hotel -- agreed in 1998 to reduce night lighting at their

Domestic livestock such as cattle can swap diseases with wild ungulates

to places where they never existed before. Domestic livestock also help to spread disease and parasites. Elk, in turn, sometimes spread parasites back to livestock.

Brucellosis

If there is one bacterial disease that keeps ranchers awake at night, it's brucellosis. Also known as Bang's disease or spontaneous abortion, the cattle version of this disease causes cows to abort their calves or give birth to calves that die soon. The cattle industry has spent hundreds of millions of dollars to eliminate brucellosis and they're dead serious: if a rancher finds brucellosis in even a single cow, state or provincial agricultural authorities kill the entire herd. Bovine brucellosis has become extremely rare in North America as a result of this strict hygiene program. "Brucellosis-free" status is important to states and countries that earn it, because it ensures open

markets for meat and live cattle.

Wild bison in Yellowstone and Wood Buffalo national parks still carry brucellosis but biologists have never found an instance of wild bison transmitting brucellosis to domestic cattle under natural conditions. Even so, that has not stopped farm bureaus and agricultural agencies from lobbying for eradication of national park bison.

Elk populations, too, can serve as reservoirs for the brucellosis bacterium. By far the most heavily infected herds are those that concentrate on artificial feeding grounds at Jackson Hole, Green River and other areas. There, the elk are forced into sustained close-quarters contact with one another. Cows who abort their calves on the feeding lines expose other elk to the infected remains. Under more natural circumstances an aborted calf would be cleaned up by coy-

otes, ravens and other scavengers before other elk encountered it. Because unnatural crowding plays an important role in the spread of this and other bacteria, there have been several outbreaks of brucellosis on commercial game farms too.

Brucellosis probably rarely, if ever, spreads from elk to cattle. In most parts of the Rocky Mountain west, elk and cattle are separate during late winter and the spring calving season when the risks of brucellosis transmission are highest. Where wild predators are available to kill and dispose of sick individuals, and where scavenging animals such as coyotes, ravens and magpies are common, elk do not appear to experience outbreaks of brucellosis.

Giant Liver Fluke

The liver fluke is a jelly-like, nearly transparent parasite that lives in the liver of elk, cattle and other animals. The fluke migrates about in the liver, destroying tissue. Sometimes its infected host's body fights back by trapping it in a chamber of hardened tissue. Elk cope better than other ungulates with liver fluke infections. Heavily infected animals, however, can die or succumb to other diseases while in their weakened state. Liver flukes are harmless to humans and, for those inclined that way, are safe to eat.

The giant liver fluke is more common in the northern Rockies than farther south. It may be more widespread than it used to be, thanks to conservation programs that transplant elk from one area to another. Transplanted animals bring their diseases and parasites with them. When wardens slaughtered elk in Banff National Park during the mid 1940s, they found no evidence of liver flukes. By the 1960s, however, liver fluke infection was common and by the late 1980s Banff elk contained an

Home is a Carcass

Even a rotting carcass is habitat where some creatures are concerned. Entomologists from Montana State University examined an elk carcass to find out what lived in it. They found more than 400 species of beetles alone. Unexpectedly, one of the most common species was a European beetle released earlier in the century as a biological control agent for agricultural crop pests. In its new home, it has become a scavenger species, joining the many hundreds of insects, birds and mammals who thrive on the remains of elk and deer.

average of 88 flukes each.

Giant liver flukes only live part of their lives inside large grazing animals. Fluke eggs find their way into the droppings of elk and other host animals. After hatching from the eggs, minute larvae swim about in water pools, eventually finding their ways into snails. There they develop cysts that the snails deposit onto grass and other plants. Grazing elk swallow the cysts and the whole cycle continues again. Because snails thrive best in wet weather, rainy years may result in more infected elk. For the same reason, giant liver flukes are more likely to infect elk that graze in wetlands.

Lungworm

Many elk populations in western North America support the thread lungworm. This parasite lives inside the lining of the lungs and the diaphragm. Infected elk develop emphysema and cough up bloody foam. Lungworms can kill infected elk, especially when already weakened by severe winter weather, overgrazing, tick infestations or crowding. The disease often peaks in early spring. Like other parasites, lungworm infection rates are highest where elk are forced to congregate on artificial feeding grounds. Biologists found that four out of five National Elk Refuge elk contained lungworms in the late 1970s. Domestic cattle commonly pass lungworms to elk.

Hydatid Tapeworm

Often called *Echinococcus*, this parasitic worm infects both elk and the animals that eat elk. In the gut of a wolf or coyote, the hydatid tapeworm

reaches full maturity. Its eggs, deposited in wolf or coyote scats, are extremely dangerous to humans. The larvae hatch inside the body of an animal that has eaten or inhaled them. They then migrate around in the new host's heart, lungs, brain or other organs, destroying tissue as they go. Humans should never handle droppings of animals in the dog family—the hydatid tapeworm is fatal to us.

Biologists have found hydatid tapeworm larvae in elk in Alberta and British Columbia, where the larvae most commonly infect lungs. The larvae cause considerable damage to elk lung tissue, so that the infected animal can no longer run as fast or as long. This, of course, increases the chance that wolves or coyotes—themselves infected with a different life stage of the same parasite—will catch the weakened animal.

Tuberculosis

Once the scourge of human populations worldwide, tuberculosis (TB)—until recently—had faded into the background of public health concerns, thanks to milk pasteurization and livestock hygiene programs. TB is a deadly bacterial infection that scars lung tissue and often kills its human victims. It spreads in body fluids—milk from infected cows, spittle and blood from ungulates. Infected elk and deer exude contaminated fluid from lymph nodes all over their body, unlike humans whose symptoms are confined mostly to the respiratory system.

Game farm elk and deer have come down with the disease in many states and

provinces. From game farms, the disease has spread into some wild herds. The Alberta government, faced with an epidemic of TB on game farms, ordered the slaughter of half that province's captive elk population - 2,600 animals. Alberta taxpayers paid more than $16 million to compensate elk ranchers for their losses. A fifth of the veterinarians and others involved in the slaughter became infected and 36 needed medical treatment.

Careful herd hygiene has reduced, but not eliminated, outbreaks of TB on game farms. Mule deer in Montana became infected after the disease appeared in a nearby white-tailed deer farm. Deer feeding stations put out by northeast Michigan hunting clubs contributed to an epidemic of TB in that state's whitetails, forcing state wildlife officials to reduce the size of the herd—and ending the Michigan livestock industry's TB-free status. In 1998, Riding Mountain National Park wardens were horrified to find Manitoba elk infected with TB.

Tuberculosis in wild ungulates is ugly and easily spread, even by contact with an infected animal's hair. Anywhere the disease has shown up in wild or farmed animals, hunters should wear rubber gloves and face masks before handling any wild elk or deer.

Predation
Mountain Lions
Mountain lions are the most widespread and common predators on most western elk ranges. Even so, most studies of radio-collared mountain lions have shown that the big cats kill deer far more often than elk. Where cougars do hunt elk, bull elk make up a disproportionately large part of the overall kill. This is probably because mountain lions hunt by stalking close to their prey, then dashing out from cover. Since cow elk are normally in herds, the odds of a surprise attack paying off are lower than for the more solitary bull elk. A feeding herd of elk usually has at least a few individuals watching out for trouble. A lone bull is bound to lower his guard from time to time. In many parts of elk country, bull elk spend more time in forest than cow herds, a factor that also gives an advantage to stalking mountain lions.

Wolves
When wolves returned to the Yellowstone ecosystem in 1995, the local elk soon learned that these newcomers meant business. Given a choice, wolves often select elk over other prey. During the first winter, some wolf packs killed elk at the rate of one per day, an exceptionally high kill rate not previously recorded by biologists. Like other predators, wolves engage in "surplus killing" when conditions are right—and on Yellowstone's northern range conditions were right. The elk were naïve and overabundant, and the winter snows deep. Biologists reported seeing wolves caching meat from their kills for later consumption. During the first spring three different females in one wolf pack produced litters of young—another indication of how predators can respond to unprece-

dented food abundance.

Yellowstone's elk are no longer complacent or naive, and Yellowstone's new wolves have to work harder now for their meals. The system has begun to adjust. As wolves continue to reduce elk numbers and elk continue to redistribute themselves in response to harassment by wolves, ecologists predict other changes will appear on the northern range. Already, scavenging birds such as magpies and ravens have re-learned old habits of monitoring wolf behavior. Soon, changes in vegetation may appear too. Overgrazed grasslands will begin to recover and aspen thickets—almost eradicated by heavy browsing—resprout.

Wolf packs commonly "test" herds of elk by approaching them slowly and alertly, watching for any chance to isolate a vulnerable individual. Most wolf kills are yearlings or calves because smaller animals are easiest to catch. In spring wolves can be very effective predators on calf elk, hunting them like bird dogs. Since wolves kill their prey by pursuing animals and pulling them down, they play a valuable role in quickly removing sick elk from the herd.

Living with Elk
Agriculture
Freshly sprouted barley or oats are like ice cream to hungry elk. Ranchers in elk country resent seeing elk foraging on young crops, and for good reason: those crops cost money to produce and are already spoken for by the rancher's cows and calves. It doesn't help any to know that when the winter

winds blow a few months hence, more elk will line up to feed on stored bales of hay. Livestock ranchers and elk compete for the same forage and the same habitat. The competition isn't made any more pleasant for the rancher when dozens of hunters arrive each fall wanting to shoot those elk on private property.

Good cattle management can actually add to the rancher's problems. When cows eat grass, they stimulate new growth that is high in sugars and proteins. Attracted by the young, tender forage, elk congregate on those same pastures after the cows leave. Grasses, however, can only cope with a finite amount of grazing before their roots start to die back and they lose vigor.

Elk on their way to graze ranchers' pastures often ignore protected grassland if it

Theodore Roosevelt Memorial Ranch

Before Theodore Roosevelt became a U.S. president he was a noted hunter and outdoorsman. Early in his adult life Roosevelt took up ranching in the North Dakota badlands. Although his ranching career lasted only a couple years, it set the stage for a lasting relationship with the American West.

Half a century after Roosevelt's death, the Boone and Crockett Club immortalized its founder by establishing the 6,000-acre Theodore Roosevelt Memorial Ranch west of Choteau, Montana. The ranch contains winter range for elk and deer herds that migrate out of the Bob Marshall and Scapegoat Wildernesses each winter. Besides protecting elk habitat in perpetuity, the ranch serves an important educational role. The society manages it as a working cattle ranch, but researchers continually monitor the interactions between livestock and wildlife. So far, it appears that they are not only compatible, but can complement one another. In 1998 ranch managers Bob and Sandy Peebles calved out 127 head of cattle. That same year, over 1,500 mule deer and 300 elk wintered on or within a mile of the ranch.

Most wildlife winter range in the west is on private land used for cattle production. Demonstration projects, research and environmental education will play an important role in conserving habitat over a much larger area. The Boone and Crockett Club attaches so much importance to the program that it endows a permanent research chair at the University of Montana in Missoula to ensure that high quality scientific work will be a continuing legacy of the Theodore Roosevelt Memorial Ranch.

has not been grazed or burned for several years. Montana game managers bought wintering range for elk only to find that the elk preferred neighboring ranches. Only when they arranged for cattle to graze the wildlife refuges for part of each growing season did the elk return.

Cattle and sheep can, of course, overgraze meadows until elk can no longer find enough food. On balance, however, elk coexist well with agriculture. The challenge for ranchers, public land managers, wildlife groups and others is to work out management plans that ensure that the needs of elk, livestock, and humans complement one another. Enlightened coexistence is particularly important where ranchers rely on public lands for summer cattle grazing. Often the elk who summer on those same public lands rely on the ranchers' private lands for winter habitat—a delicate relationship that results in mutual dependence.

Elk and the Hunt

The elk, more than any game animal, represents many hunters' ideal of wilderness hunting. Generations of hunters have waited impatiently for the aspens to turn gold and the first frosts to settle on high country meadows. The smell of curing vegetation conjures up images of distant elk bugling, campfire coffee, dark timber and high ridgetops. Supplying and outfitting the annual pilgrimage of hopeful elk hunters has become a vital part of rural economies from Rifle, Colorado to Fort St. John, British Columbia.

For those who know the country well and take time to study the movements of their prey, elk are relatively easy to hunt. Still, millennia of sur-

Bob Peebles, land and wildlife manager,
Theodore Roosevelt Memorial Ranch

"*My greatest worth* here has got nothing to do with my ability to manage a ranch. The biggest asset of my work has been to promote common sense and practical solutions to the club. I'm not concerned so much with my neighbors. Most of them have been in business for well over 100 years now. They've had 10 decades to fine tune their management techniques to their land. The only things we're trying to help them with now are the changes that are coming at them in terms of philosophy. Wildlife management is one of the biggest ones. We ranchers didn't really have to think too much about wildlife until 1974 with the passage of the Endangered Species Act. That really hit home in the minds of a lot of people and instinctively caused fear. The push for endangered species caused an equal and opposite reaction, which was the push back. And when they looked at the grizzly {bear} and things like that in this area that we're dealing directly with, well then they were suddenly thrown into the rest of the arena with mule deer and sheep and goats and elk and all the rest of it.

We're not trying to create enemies here. We're just trying to create a forum for people to share information. There are so many things that involve conservation now. It's hard to stay focussed within the parameters that we need to stay focussed on here at the ranch. We have to keep within the context of wildlife-livestock interactions. There are all kinds of things that come into play around elk - mineral development, streamflow, water quality, predator control, Endangered Species Act, public lands/private lands, fee hunting versus public hunting. If you've got 10 people in the room, you can have 10 different concepts of what it is the elk do for me, and what I do for the elk."

Jack Ward Thomas

Noted elk researcher Jack Ward Thomas is a soft-spoken Texan who served for three tough years as the Chief of the U.S. Forest Service. His simple advice to forest supervisors and other staff in the controversy-plagued agency became famous: "Tell the truth and obey the law."

Dr. Thomas cautions against easy answers in the continuing debate over the appropriate use of western public lands: "In the intermountain west, public lands are the high country. That's where the elk are nine months out of the year. Then they show up on the low elevation winter ranges. Most of those are in private ownership. Most of the people where those elk winter also have grazing rights on the federal lands for which they pay a quite nominal fee. Well, the environmentalists are beating the hell out of them about their grazing on federal lands. They're not really concerned about the price. They're really interested in driving them off. They have not considered what the consequences of driving them off are.

"There's been a quid pro quo forever. Ranchers don't bitch much about those elk and deer that are wintering on their private ground if someone gives them cheap federal lands grazing. Now, it takes that federal land grazing for them to have a functional ranching unit. So if we drive them off that federal land or we increase the price of the grazing to where their marginal operations become sub-marginal, what do they do with that land? They subdivide it.

"They might hang in there for two reasons. One is their land prices are accelerating. And the other is, they've been there for generations and it's a way of life. If you looked at their circumstances and you were their financial advisor, you would almost certainly tell them to sell out. I mean, you've got a $5 million USD investment and you're making $50,000 USD a year in profit -- I mean, are you insane? Take the money and run. And more and more of them are doing that.

"Then the buyers subdivide it again, and people become less tolerant of the elk and deer. Then we get faced with, do we buy that land and put more land into federal ownership? That's not too popular. Is there enough money? The answer's no. And if we had it, well, if you live in a state or a county that's 70 or 80 percent federal ownership, the locals get a little bit hyper about any more land going out of private ownership into public ownership.

"So, be careful of what you ask for because you just might get it."

After leaving the Forest Service, Jack Ward Thomas joined the faculty of the University of Montana in Missoula, where he occupies the Theodore Roosevelt Chair in Wildlife Management.

"Our particular niche is training doctoral students to operate at the intersection of ecology, economics, sociology, and law. We were all told in school that this was 95 percent people and 5

Jack Ward Thomas

percent biology, and then they trained us in 95 percent biology and 5 percent people. So we take people who are well-qualified biologists and train them to deal with real world conservation. You can go talk to somebody until you're blue about what's good and bad, right and wrong, but pretty soon you've got to talk about feasibility.

"In class I explain it by drawing four circles that overlap. I call one circle law and I call one ecology and I call one economics and I call one social/cultural factors. Where those all overlap is where you can operate. Most of the pressures in our society are pulling these circles apart rather than pushing them together. We get more and more law that's more and more constraining, and that pulls that circle out. Most of the things we find out in ecology are not exactly liberating, so that pulls that circle out. The guy that is trying to stay in business and stay alive and pay his taxes, and that's pulling that one out.

"That's where we train students to operate, is at that intersection."

The Feedground Controversy

Wild elk are generally healthy elk

Elk have posed problems for ranchers ever since domestic cattle first arrived in the West. As farms and cattle preempted traditional wintering grounds, elk quickly learned to zero in on stored hay.

Wildlife agencies soon found themselves stuck between the desire of hunters to have abundant elk herds, and the reluctance of ranchers to feed them each winter. A popular solution was for wildlife agencies to buy tracts of marginal agricultural land and feed the elk there. The National Elk Refuge was only one of many such feeding grounds scattered from New Mexico to Idaho. Only Montana and western Canada avoided succumbing to temptation to feed wintering elk artificially.

According to Wyoming conservationist Robert Hoskin, the problem with the view that "a

bale of hay is worth an acre of habitat" is that it deprives both animals and landscape of naturalness. Feedgrounds, he points out, would not exist if commercial hunting outfitters didn't demand lots of elk, and commercial livestock ranchers didn't insist those elk be confined on small parts of the landscape.

"The fundamental problem that elk feedgrounds pose," says Hoskin, "is that they reflect 'agricultural production' attitudes toward land and wildlife that necessarily contradict the goals of wildlife conservation. Feedgrounds are a symptom of a much larger shift in 20th century North America from elk and other wildlife as wild, to wildlife as domesticated commodities."

More than half a century ago the father of wildlife management, Aldo Leopold waded into the debate over artificial winter

feeding when he asserted that "... the value of a head of game is inverse to the intensity of the management system that produced it." By Leopold's standard, feedgrounds devalue elk by turning them, at least seasonally, into semi-tame livestock.

Controversy over feedgrounds —especially their role in spreading diseases such as brucellosis, tuberculosis and chronic wasting disease—led the Wyoming Wildlife Federation to organize a well-attended conference on feedgrounds in 1998. Most who attended felt that elk fare best when wild and free. Protecting natural winter range for elk, most biologists agree, is better in the long term than confining them to tiny pieces of the landscape and training them to eat alfalfa pellets.

vival in a world of predators have made elk quick to learn and adjust to the behavior of predators—humans included. Most elk fall prey to hunters during the first two or three days of the hunting season. After that, elk avoid roads, become increasingly nocturnal, and spend more time in forested cover. Successful hunters often watch likely feeding areas at dawn or dusk to locate elk herds, then stalk carefully to within shooting range.

Many hunting seasons correspond with the rut, when elk are still on their summer range. Hunters may have to hike, ride or be packed into remote backcountry to find their quarry. Where elk numbers are chronically higher than winter range can support, wildlife managers sometimes schedule late season hunts to make it

easier for hunters to find elk after they've migrated out of the high country.

Elk meat is lean and healthy, and it tastes good. Laws require even trophy hunters, motivated mostly by the desire to find the largest and most spectacular bull elk, to salvage all the meat. Hunters who would waste elk meat are rare. For many hunters, feeding their families elk meat is an affirmation of their identity—each meal becomes a celebration of the West's natural diversity and a ceremonial way of becoming more at one with the living world. You are, after all, what you eat.

Wildlife managers view elk hunting in a more prosaic light; they see it as a way to manage elk herds. All animals that evolved in the presence of predators are also highly pro-

ductive to compensate for losses. Without predators they can overpopulate their habitat. Regulated hunting normally keeps elk numbers from growing too large for their winter ranges. It also helps ensure the tolerance of ranchers who must cope with the impact of elk grazing on their crops and forage supplies. However, some Colorado and Montana elk herds have become so large—and so good at recognizing private ranch land as safe terrain—that state wildlife agencies no longer can sell enough hunting tags to keep elk numbers under control.

Rocky Mountain Elk Foundation

One of the largest habitat conservation organizations in western North America began in Troy, Montana, in 1984. Like so many others, the Rocky Mountain Elk Foundation (RMEF) was born out of the desire of a group of hunters to give something back to animals and wild places. From its original four members, RMEF has grown to include more than 110,000 people committed to: "...ensure the future of elk, other wildlife and their habitat."

RMEF has raised more than $75 million USD for elk habitat. Members donate out of their own pockets or organize fund raising banquets that feature auctions of donated wildlife art, outfitted hunts and merchandise. In 1996 alone, banquets generated

more than $10 million USD. Some of the money goes to support elk research or projects to return elk to ancestral homes. In 1995 and 1996, for example, the organization helped restore elk to northern Wisconsin and Tennessee's Land Between the Lakes.

Most, however, goes to protect critical elk habitat.

Sometimes RMEF buys land outright when imminent sale to developers threatens elk habitat. Usually, however, the association prefers to stretch their dollars by purchasing only the development rights to land. Conservation easements—legal restrictions attached to the land title—are less expensive than outright purchase. Most conservation easements permit

existing uses of the land such as ranching and hunting but protect it from subdivision, road development or habitat destruction. RMEF holds easements on almost 100,000 acres of habitat from New Mexico to Alberta.

Habitat protection is an investment in the future. So is education - so the Elk Foundation publishes an award winning children's magazine—*Wild Outdoor World*—and an insightful magazine for all members—*Bugle*. In addition it has a large interpretive center at its international headquarters in Missoula, Montana.

For more information call (800) CALLELK or key into www.rmef.org on the internet.

Right: Antler-rubbing bull elk

Mule Deer
(Odocoileus hemionus)

Mule deer bucks

L ike wind, space and rugged scenery, mule deer are fundamental elements of the North American West. Even before the game slaughters of the 19th century, mule deer rarely wandered east of the Great Plains—they simply weren't at home in well-wooded country.

"Mulies" live along the edges of the big open, wherever canyons, coulees, mountainsides or foothills offer the steep terrain they need to elude predators.

Open country has shaped much of the mule deer's behavior. Mule deer stand and watch approaching predators. When scared, they usually run a short distance uphill only to stop and watch again. Whitetails, on the other hand, are forest deer. They escape predators by fleeing rapidly, often downhill, into the security of dense cover. Only after their initial pell-mell flight do they stop to watch and smell their backtrail.

Mule deer rely on their ability to move rapidly over rough terrain, rarely exerting themselves any more than absolutely necessary to put a safe distance between themselves and their pursuers. When pressed, a mule deer breaks into a bouncing gait as if it were on a pogo-stick. This "stotting" is inefficient on flat terrain or in dense forest, but enables the deer quickly to move up or down steep slopes in full control and with little waste of energy. Ernest Thompson Seton describes watching three hounds almost overtake a doe and fawns on an open river flat. When the deer turned and went up the valley slope, the dogs fell hopelessly behind.

Stotting allows mule deer to change direction rapidly and even reverse themselves if necessary. It also enables them to bound through burned forests crisscrossed with deadfall, while pursuing predators must find their way over and around the tangle of downed logs.

Mule deer developed their behavior in response to their open country habitat and the hunting strategies of their predators—wolves, cougars and coyotes prefer surprise attacks to extended chases. Aboriginal hunters, too, because of their low technology weaponry, needed to be close to deer before they could kill them.

Once deer predators began to pack guns, however, habits that had served mule deer well for thousands of years became liabilities. Standing deer are easier to aim at than running ones. Until game laws and an accompanying change in hunter ethics offered respite, the big western deer died by the thousands. Some accessible herds didn't recover from overhunting until well into the middle of the 20th century.

John M. Murphy, writing in 1879, reported that three men killed 1,500 deer, mostly mule deer, in the Judith River basin over a period of six weeks. They took the skins and left the carcasses to rot. "I heard of a man who killed over a hundred in one stand in a mountain pass in Colorado...This ruthless destruction is producing the most disastrous results, for where mule deer were so plentiful in 1868 that they could be seen by the hundred in a march of twenty-four hours, scarcely a dozen could be seen in the same region in 1877."

Ernest Thompson Seton, in 1909, wrote that "...in the later 80's the winter haunts of the Blacktail [mule deer] in southern British Columbia were invaded by skin hunters. Thousands of the hides were sold at 25 cents a piece and the meat left in the woods to rot—a shameless destruction."

Game regulations that lumped easily-killed mule deer with the more elusive whitetail kept mule deer scarce in much of prairie Canada until the 1970s. In the U.S. west, however, mule deer numbers rebounded rapidly once regulations controlled hunter kill. Deer herds peaked in the 1960s and have declined gradually ever since.

The long-term prognosis for mule deer is bad. Valerius Geist, in his book Mule Deer Country, describes the mule deer as "a species marked for extinction." Biologists, hunters, ranchers and environmental groups continue to debate the reasons for mule

Mule Deer Facts

Length:
bucks: 125-175 cm. (4-5.5 ft.)
does: 100-150 cm. (3.5-5 ft.)

Weight:
bucks: 100-180 kg. (220-400 lbs.)
does: 50-125 kg. (110-275 lbs)

Description:
Reddish-brown in summer; grey in winter. White rump patch with a black-tipped, ropy white tail. Fawns are brown with white spots. Bucks have black foreheads and antlers that fork repeatedly, spreading out laterally from the head rather than forward along it. Mule deer earned their common name from their distinctive large ears. When startled they bound with all four feet in a pogo-stick like "stotting" gait.

Life Span:
Up to 22 years (does) or 16 years (bucks); most live less than ten years.

Reproduction:
First breed at a year old on good range; otherwise at two. Twin fawns are usual; triplets are rare. Yearling does and does on poor range may produce single fawns.

Food:
Forbs and leaves in summer; fallen leaves, buds and evergreen plants in winter.

Distribution:
Mountains, deserts and prairie regions of western North America from southern Yukon, northern B.C. and Alberta south to Mexico and Texas, and east to Manitoba and parts of the Mississippi drainage. Black-tailed deer, a group of closely related subspecies, live along the Pacific coast drainages from California to southern Alaska.

Mule deer in snow

Black-tailed Deer

From southern Alaska along the Pacific Rim to southern California, smaller relatives of the mule deer leave their tracks on windswept beaches, shelter under rainforests of red cedar and Sitka spruce, and fatten in the lush alpine meadows of the coastal mountain ranges.

The black-tailed deer has been around far longer than the mule deer. Most taxonomists believe that blacktails evolved from primitive white-tailed deer that became isolated along the Pacific Coast during the Pleistocene era. The rainy, lush and often precipitous terrain supports forests of giant evergreens far different from the deciduous eastern woodlands where whitetails evolved. As deer adapted to this unique environment, they came to look and behave unlike their relatives thousands of miles to the east.

By the end of the last great continental ice age—about 10-14,000 years ago—the black-tailed deer had become a distinct new species. Unlike whitetails whose antlers normally sweep forward, with secondary tines emerging in a row along the top,

blacktail antlers branch into two main tines that each then branch again. In this regard, blacktail antlers are similar to—but smaller than—mule deer antlers.

Blacktails lack the large white rump patch of mule deer. They don't have brown tails like whitetails either—nor do they raise their tail and flag the white underside when startled. Alaskan blacktails have a brown tail with a black tip. More southerly blacktails have black lines down the top of their tail and a black tip.

Because of their small size and lush coastal habitats, blacktails can become very abundant. The most productive habitat—if interspersed with old-growth forest—is where logging or fire opens up the rainforest and lets lush deciduous shrubbery take over. Many herds winter along river bottoms and in coastal forests, but migrate up into coastal mountains in summer to take advantage of green timberline meadows. Snowfall in those mountains can be extremely heavy in winter because of the amount of moisture sweeping inland from the Pacific Ocean. In

Washington, B.C. and Alaska, old-growth forest stands whose tree canopies intercept snow are vitally important for wintering blacktails and their larger relatives, the Roosevelt elk..

Biologists believe the mule deer is a hybrid species that resulted from blacktail bucks mating with whitetail does. This became possible only after melting glaciers allowed blacktails to spread east and whitetails to spread west into mountainous country.

DNA evidence supports the theory. Mitochondria—tiny energy-producing organelles found inside each living cell—have different DNA from the cell nucleus. While half the DNA in a cell's nucleus comes from an animal's father and half from its mother, all mitochondrial DNA comes from the mother.

Black-tailed deer and whitetails have different mitochondrial DNA, while mule deer mitochondrial DNA is similar to that of whitetails—evidence that female whitetails must have been involved, fairly recently, in the evolution of the mule deer.

deer decline. In truth, it's probably a combination of habitat change, expanding populations of elk and white-tailed deer, and predation - both human and four-legged.

Mule Deer Habitat

Unlike whitetails, most mule deer migrate between summer and winter ranges. Whatever the season, however, mule deer like semi-open, broken country where forest, shrubbery and meadow intermingle. Mule deer graze on open slopes, especially in winter and spring. Brushy slopes full of serviceberry (saskatoon), willow, rose and, farther south, bitterbrush and maple are great habitat—they offer both abundant browse and hiding cover. Deer often bed in sheltered locations under rimrock or coniferous trees to avoid wind, summer sun, rain and the watchful eyes of predators. In winter, on the other hand, mule deer take advantage of sun-exposed south facing slopes to soak up what little warmth is available at that season.

Mule Deer Food

There really isn't much a mule deer won't eat at one time or another. Naturalists have even seen mule deer eating fish and mice, although these were exceptional cases. For the most part, mule deer forage on whatever plants are most nutritious and accessible from one week to the next. Their diverse feeding habits mean that various habitats become important at different times of the year.

Wintering mule deer eat dead leaves and partially-cured vegetation that they dig

Glow-in-the-Dark Deer?

In the deep snow country of coastal British Columbia, Washington and Oregon, black-tailed deer and Roosevelt elk need old-growth forests for winter survival. The tall trees intercept snow that would otherwise accumulate on the ground and trap the ungulates.

But there's another reason old-growth forest is important to wintering ungulates. As snow and frost build up on the lichen-festooned branches of the old trees, some of those branches break off and fall on top of the snow. The lichens—some look like dense mats of scraggly hair and others like crusty mud—are rich in carbohydrates. At a season when snow covers other plants, lichens can be vital survival food for hungry ungulates.

Lichen grows slowly, so it is scarce in young forests. The abundant lichens of ancient rainforests are slow to grow back after logging—one of many good reasons to protect old-growth.

Feeding on lichens has a downside, however. Unlike other plants, lichens concentrate airborne contaminants -- particularly radioactive fallout. In the 1960s, when the superpowers were still testing atomic weapons above ground, an Alaska researcher found that lichens had 10 to 100 times more radioactive strontium-90 and cesium-137 than other plants. Caribou that fed on those lichens had 25 to 30 times more radioactivity in their flesh than meat from other animals.

Hunters and other predators

hemlock and lichen

who regularly eat deer or other animals that feed on lichens may, consequently, have a serious personal stake in the continued effectiveness of atomic test ban treaties.

from beneath the snow. They also paw down to find evergreen plants such as juniper. Ice and wind storms, by breaking off the top branches of poplars or firs, provide windfalls of forage that deer otherwise would be unable to reach.

In late winter, mule deer rely heavily on the buds and young twigs of low-growing shrubs and trees such as serviceberry, aspen, willow and big sagebrush, which are only available to them where snow remains shallow. Large herds of mule deer often congregate on ranchers' hayfields to eat alfalfa that is frozen green. In severe winters, deer can become a serious problem when they invade feedyards and destroy baled hay. Deer cannot switch rapidly from one food type to another, because the bacteria in their rumens need time to adjust.

The first signs of spring in mule deer country are often grassy openings on south facing slopes where sun and wind melt openings in the snowpack. Deer congregate on these exposed hillsides to feed on the first green blades of grass and other plants. In March and April deer are at their most desperate, having lost weight throughout the long winter while they ate woody browse of low quality. As a result, these low elevation, sun-exposed slopes are critical habitat. When humans expropriate them for mines, recreational homes or highways, mule deer populations suffer.

Some plants seem to appeal to deer only if they can mix them with others. For instance, researchers found that mule deer avoid pure sagebrush. On the other hand, if they can add bitterbrush and other shrubs to their daily diet, they will eat large amounts of sage. Overpopulated winter ranges soon run out of the more palatable shrubs. When that happens, the abundant sage ceases to be useful food, and deer begin to starve amid seeming plenty.

Deer eat far more kinds of plants than they avoid. One Utah study found mule deer to eat 125 different species. Even so, the deer concentrated on only eight species for most of their diet. Colorado mule deer preferred only 10 species of the dozens available to them. Of those, serviceberry, chokecherry and oak were by far the most important—accounting for almost 90 percent of their diet.

Well-fed deer with nutritious diets grow to maturity faster, accumulate more fat and are stronger at the onset of winter, can withstand disease and parasites better, produce more and healthier young, and are best able to avoid predators. Little wonder that most deer, when you see them, are chewing on something.

Water

Drought is a fact of life west of the 100th meridian. Every living thing must adapt to the reality that western water is always scarce and sometimes runs out. Most life concentrates near streams and perennial wetlands. Elsewhere, the distribution of water in the landscape limits both vegetation density and wildlife abundance.

Some animals, such as kangaroo rats and kit foxes, can get all the water they need from the foods they eat—as long as they are careful. Mule deer, however, have to be able to find drinking water, especially during hot weather. Mule deer in Arizona need twice as much water in summer as in winter. Where succulent forage is abundant it provides some moisture, but the availability of drinking water—springs, seeps, perennial streams or tanks that trap rainwater—is what makes or breaks desert deer. Many deer simply abandon the hot summer desert and travel up into the mountains where water is more abundant.

In winter, snow works just as well—wintering deer often eat snow rather than look for open water. Dry, cold winters can be nearly as hard on northern mule deer as dry summers are on desert deer. Polluted water sources can be almost as bad as no water at all. Several studies have shown that disease and fawn mortality increase when water holes are shallow, muddy and trampled by deer and livestock.

Security

Security for a mule deer may consist of steep, rocky terrain in a canyon or on a mountainside, or dense shrubby cover. Mule deer rely on their eyes and nose to watch out for trouble, so they often bed below rimrock or among scattered conifers where broken shade conceals them while they look out over the landscape below. When danger threatens the deer may flee into more broken terrain or

Kaibab Plateau

Grand Canyon

Wildlife conservationists learned a hard lesson in range ecology and the importance of predators when they decided to protect a popular mule deer herd in northern Arizona. Set aside in 1906, the Grand Canyon National Game Preserve included most of the Kaibab National Forest north of the Grand Canyon. Wildlife officials estimated that nearly 3,000 mule deer summered in the plateau's ponderosa pine forests and wintered to the east in pinyon/juniper stands along the edges of the canyon.

The prescription for protecting the mule deer population was straightforward: make sure nothing kills any deer, and reduce competition for forage. Wardens aggressively enforced the total ban on hunting. Government hunters killed 674 mountain lions, eleven wolves, at least 3,000 coyotes and more than 120 bobcats between 1906 and 1923. The refuge managers also reduced the number of domestic livestock on the preserve from 15,000 cattle to 5,400, and 9,000 sheep to 3,650.

The deer population exploded. By 1922, biologists estimated it at 20,000. Two years later some estimates ran as high as 100,000. Deer were everywhere and visitors were delighted. But biologists quickly saw the consequences of a deer herd deprived of its predators. Junipers were high lined -- stripped of foliage from the ground up. Most of the forest understory died of too many nips. Aspen forests began to fail, with young aspens browsed as soon as they sprouted and the mature trees stripped of their bark as high as a starving deer could reach on its hind legs. Eroding deer trails wrinkled the canyon slopes.

A special commission assigned to investigate the growing disaster in 1924 called for cutting the size of the herd in half. They proposed trapping some deer and shipping them to understocked ranges elsewhere. Hunters should remove the rest or, if that seemed undesirable, the commission suggested a controlled slaughter. When the game preserve opened to hunting that fall, hunters shot 400 deer but outraged citizens insisted that

managers leave the deer alone and let nature regulate their numbers.

As the debate raged, even famous western writer Zane Grey weighed in. He proposed to help the government organize volunteers to drive at least 5,000 deer across the Grand Canyon to the south rim. The idea caught on, and in 1925 a long line of cowboys, Navajos and altruistic visitors spread out to drive deer to the canyon rim. When the dust settled, the drivers had failed to herd even one deer down into the canyon.

The winter of 1925/26 saw a massive die-off of mule deer as starvation and severe winter took its toll of the overcrowded herd. Die-offs continued annually until 1930. Today, forest managers again tolerate cougars and coyotes in the Kaibab National Forest, as well as an annual influx of human hunters. Mule deer are no longer cursed by too much safety. More than half a century later, the forests have almost finished recovering from a badly flawed experiment in deer management.

shoot coyotes as a matter of policy, mule deer often congregated near park highways where coyotes dared not linger.

Shelter

Shelter protects deer from predators and weather. Coniferous timber is particularly valuable in winter since the dark evergreen needles absorb warmth from the sun, and the heavy forest canopy blocks cold winds and keeps deer hidden from danger. On windy days, deer use topography for shelter too, feeding and bedding on the leeward side of hogbacks and ridges.

Deer need shelter not only in winter but during the heat of summer too. In many parts of the west, mule deer migrate up to high elevation summer ranges where they can avoid the oppressive heat of the valley bottoms. On hot days, mule deer often bed down on shady north-facing slopes or take shelter in dense evergreen thickets where they can avoid the hot sun. Some particularly favorable bedding areas under overhanging rocks or on isolated ledges or knolls develop deeply worn beds littered with the droppings of generations of deer.

Mule deer doe and fawn grooming one another

quietly bury themselves in shrubbery. Above timberline or on the rolling plains east of the Rockies, mule deer sometimes bed well out in the open

where they can spot approaching predators far off.

When cougars, wolves or humans put local populations of mule deer under sustained pressure, the deer often retreat to more secure habitat. Mule deer wintering in the Waterton Lakes National Park townsite, for instance, moved out of town for several weeks when a female cougar and her kittens moved in. Heavily hunted mule deer avoid the vicinity of roads so consistently that their habitat's carrying capacity shrinks as new forest or mineral development roads go in. On the other hand, when national park wardens used to

Mule Deer Family Life

Fawns hide by lying flat. Some biologists say a lack of body scent protects fawns from the sharp noses of hunting predators, but their behavior likely plays the biggest role in saving them. A small animal lying very still releases little body odor. Remaining close to the ground in vegetation keeps

High-Test Fawn Fuel

Deer udders are small compared to cow udders. Deer milk makes up in quality what it lacks in quantity, however: it has about three times as much fat and protein as cow milk. Does put so much of their own energy into producing good milk that their coats become dull and ratty compared to other deer.

what odor that does escape from being caught by the wind. Predators that rely on sound, sight and scent to find prey are at a disadvantage when hunting stationary fawns.

Doe mule deer give birth in late May or early June. A doe separates herself from other deer and retires to a sheltered place. After delivering one or two tiny fawns—about the size of a shoebox - the doe eats the afterbirth and any vegetation soiled by blood or other birth fluids. She also cleans the fawns thoroughly with her tongue, ensuring that as few

odors as possible remain to attract predators. Usually the gangly newborn fawns follow their mother a short distance before lying down and hiding while she wanders off to feed.

Does spend very little time with their fawns at first, returning only occasionally to nurse and clean them. This keeps noise, activity and odors to a minimum near the fawns and improves their chance of surviving the vulnerable first weeks of life. Fawns and does communicate with low bleats and buzzing noises. After about two weeks, fawns become strong enough to follow

their mothers around. If a predator or human startles them, the fawns often drop flat on the ground and lie still while their mother turns to face the intruder. Mule deer mothers have a strong mobbing instinct, especially while their fawns are young. They readily attack coyotes, domestic dogs and even black bears with their front hooves. A doe will often hurry from a considerable distance, ears cupped forward and head low, to attack a predator. Humans walking dogs on leashes have learned the hard way that a mother mule deer's unprovoked fury can result in an unplanned visit to the vet, or worse.

Fawns taste their first green food soon after they begin to accompany their mother, but they continue to nurse sometimes as late as October or November. Once the fawns are mobile, their mothers begin to spend more time in herds of does and yearlings.

A fawn's two most dangerous times are immediately after birth when it is helpless against predators, and again during its first winter. Fawns grow rapidly through the summer and fall, but they still go into the winter half the size of their mothers. Their small bodies have a higher ratio of surface area—where heat escapes—to body mass—where heat is stored—than larger deer. Their short legs also put them at a disadvantage for dealing with deep snow. Fawns and small yearlings are often the first to succumb to a hard winter or to fall prey to predators who are always on the lookout for weakness.

Lost Fawns

Young fawns lie very still for safety

Every year people find fawns that seem abandoned or lost. The temptation to save the fragile little creatures is hard to resist. Unfortunately, rescuing fawns does more harm than good. Adopted fawns usually die. Those that survive can become aggressive and dangerous.

The best treatment for a lost fawn is to leave it alone. Usually, in fact, its mother has not actually abandoned it. A doe leaves her fawn alone because remaining nearby could draw the attention of predators. Instead, the mother feeds at a safe distance, sneaking back from time to time to nurse her little one before leaving again to refill herself. If a kindly human finds the fawn during her absence and pats or holds the little animal, the result is simply to cover it and its bedding area with human scent that can draw curious predators near. The kindest thing is simply to walk away from it.

Left: Mule deer buck

Mule Deer Social Life

Mule deer society is more complex than it appears to we who only peer into it from time to time. Some deer are influential and important, while others have to submit to frequent bullying. Young deer defer to their more seasoned elders. Some find the rigid dominance structure of the herd too confining and wander off to explore on their own. Strangers show off to one another and sometimes fight to establish status. Does babysit. Fawns play chasing games and "king of the castle." A herd of mule deer grazing in a meadow is far more than it appears—it is a society of animals who use scents, sounds and body language to establish and maintain complex relationships with one another.

With mule deer, as with most animals, staring another animal in the eye is an act of aggression. Only the dominant deer in any given herd can make eye contact with other deer and not expect an aggressive response. As a result, mule deer usually face more or less in the same direction when feeding, and lie down facing away from one another. Of course, this behavior has another advantage—it means the herd can watch for danger from all directions. Deer who know one another try to reduce stress by constantly reassuring each other through their body language that they mean no harm. Mule deer often avert their eyes, lay their ears back, lower their heads and assume a crouching posture—all in the interests of letting the other deer know they

want no conflict.

When a deer feels affronted by another's behavior, it may become aggressive to reassert its status in the herd. It might strike the offending deer with a front leg, or raise its head and rise on its hind legs as if it means to kick. Aggressive deer often spread their ears wide and lower them, turn their bodies sideways to their opponent, and stare at the deer they wish to intimidate. This is similar to the posture deer assume when "mobbing" predators such as coyotes or dogs. These dominance displays let deer constantly reassert their status without wasting energy or risking injury through open combat.

In the rare cases when dominance displays fail, doe

mule deer fight by rearing up on their hind legs and flailing at one another with dangerously-sharp front hooves.

Buck mule deer have an additional set of tools for sorting out status—their antlers. Except during the rut and winter, buck mule deer usually associate with other bucks. In these bachelor herds every buck knows his place because of frequent gentle pushing matches and other interactions that establish which buck is strongest. Large antlers and heavy bodies indicate maturity and vigor, so bucks often stretch out their necks and display their size as they walk in front of one another.

Mule Deer/Whitetail Hybrids

Biologist Valerius Geist blames it on poorly designed hunting regulations in places where white-tailed deer and mule deer coexist. Wherever generous bag limits make it possible for hunters to kill most of the mature mule deer bucks, the risk of hybridization between whitetails and mule deer increases. Geist theorizes that large mature mule deer bucks can normally find and breed does. In their absence, however, aggressive white-tailed bucks take over the role, easily displacing the few small mule deer bucks that survive.

Hybridization works against the mule deer population in the long run, since the offspring are incompetent animals who rarely survive. Researcher Susan Lingle found that hybrid deer neither

bolt for cover like a whitetail, nor stot uphill out of danger's way or mob predators like a mule deer. Instead, they act indecisive and confused. A doe that produces a hybrid fawn is unlikely to become a grandmother.

Geist suspects that this kind of hybridization may be partly to blame for the decline in mule deer numbers in some parts of the West. The obvious solution: redesign hunting seasons to protect mature mule deer bucks and give them a chance to breed undisturbed during the rut. Few game commissions or politicians like that idea, however. It could mean fewer hunters in the field for shorter periods - fewer happy voters. The alternative, however, may be the demise of mule deer from many parts of their range.

Mule deer bucks sort out most conflicts without fighting.

Mule Deer Rutting Season

During the rut, or breeding season, the stakes become higher in social interactions between bucks. Intense conflicts can result. Rutting bucks are full of testosterone, a male sex hormone that affects both their temperaments and body shapes. The heavy swollen necks of rutting mule deer bucks, which give them a more impressive profile when they display to one another, is a product of testosterone's effects on their body. If two bucks meet at this season, the larger body of the dominant buck usually intimidates his smaller rival. If the bucks are near the same size, however, a serious fight may result with both bucks locking antlers, twisting and trying to throw one another off balance. Very rarely, fighting mule deer will get their antlers locked, so that both die slow deaths of stress and starvation. Less uncommonly, one or both bucks sustain puncture wounds to their bodies. Perhaps because of these risks, rutting mule deer

sort out most conflicts without resorting to full-fledged fighting.

Unlike elk, mule deer bucks do not gather harems of does and keep them together until each doe has come into estrous. A large, dominant buck might control access to a doe herd, but he does nothing to try and keep the does together; instead, he concentrates on keeping other large bucks away. Most bucks travel from one group of does to another. When a buck encounters a doe that may be ready to breed he tends her closely. Dr. Valerius Geist, a specialist in ungulate behavior, believes that buck mule deers act almost baby-like to avoid alienating the object of their affections. Buck mule deer have similar face markings to young fawns. They bleat like fawns and avoid direct eye contact.

Does show their reproductive state chemically, as the concentrations of various hormones and other substances in their urine changes. A buck checks to see if a doe is ready to mate by stretching out his neck, approaching the doe

from the rear, making a low buzzing noise, and licking at her flanks. Eventually, the doe urinates and the buck moves in to taste the urine. Like some other animals—including some cats—bucks have a specialized organ in the top of their mouth. The Jacobson's organ is extremely sensitive to small amounts of chemicals. After tasting the doe's urine the buck curls back his lips, arches his neck, and remains stationary for several seconds. This "lip-curl" apparently draws the urine across his Jacobson's organ.

Sometimes a rutting buck will charge a doe, grunting and thumping the feet with his hooves, to stimulate her to urinate. Does can get so weary of harassment by an eager buck that they will walk into dense bushes where the buck's antlers stop him from following, or lie flat on the ground where he can't sniff their nether regions.

A dominant mule deer buck may mate with several does over two or three weeks of intense activity.

Mule deer

Mule Deer Through the Seasons

Mule deer begin to disperse from their winter ranges in April, breaking into smaller groups and following the retreating snowpack to higher elevations. Unlike the fall migration that may bring deer en masse to their winter ranges over a period of only a few days, the return to summer range can drag on for weeks. By late May, however, with spring's greenery at its most lush and palatable, does retire to secluded thickets on their summer ranges to give birth to fawns. In herds where bucks are over hunted or rutting season frequently interrupted, some fawns may not be born until well into July. This puts them at a serious disadvantage the following winter since they have only a few weeks to grow before food quality declines and the cold winds begin to blow.

Summer is a season of abundance for most mule deer. Vegetation is abundant and the entire landscape is accessible. Water, however, can be a problem in some parts of the west. Desert mule deer, in fact, may thrive better in winter than during the dry summer months when vegetation goes dormant and water supplies dwindle.

Fawns grow rapidly. Most lose their spots by late summer and with their mothers they join other doe-fawn pairs to form small herds. As summer progresses the deer feed more on leaves and less on grasses. The bucks, having shed the velvet that covered their growing antlers in spring and early summer, spend a great deal of time testing one another's strength and feeding. In late October mule deer begin to drift toward their rutting ranges and bucks become increasingly interested in the doe-fawn herds.

Mule deer rut in November—when they are fat from summer's green abundance and before winter has begun to sap their energy. In national parks and roadless wilderness areas, most does become pregnant during their first estrous period. Where mule deer face heavy hunting pressure in November or where bucks are much scarcer than does, however, many does go through their first estrous cycle without getting bred. Yearling does may also fail to breed during the November rut. When this happens, the unbred does come into estrous three to four weeks later and a second, less-intense, rutting season results. Some does may even have to wait another four weeks, until mid January, before a buck finally breeds them.

After the rut, bucks become solitary or form into small bachelor herds. They often retreat to heavy cover and become somewhat sedentary. The does form larger groups. Large bucks shed their antlers in midwinter and sometimes then join the doe herds. Smaller bucks retain their antlers up to several weeks longer. Through the long months of winter, mule deer concentrate on saving energy

Coyotes can be efficient fawn predators

and finding food. They congregate in shallow snow areas—often south-facing slopes—and eat the buds and young twigs of various wild shrubs.

Late in the winter the lengthening hours of sunlight melt snow from south exposures and produce the first green grasses. Having starved for several months, mule deer gravitate to the new greenery. As spring progresses, more vegetation begins to green up and the melting snow opens more landscape to travel.

Don't Feed the Deer

As early as 1971, biologist William Dasmann argued against the practice of feeding deer during hard winters. He argued that starvation and winterkill are Nature's inelegant but effective way of keeping deer from becoming so abundant that they damage the vegetation that feeds them.

"Supplemental feeding removes this natural check," he wrote in *If Deer are to Survive*. "If it is successful, more deer are carried through the winter to exert further pressures on the native plants. Heavier supplemental rations then will be needed...Eventually, when natural forage plants are destroyed, the deer will become entirely dependent on artificial foods."

Most emergency feeding programs are designed to fail in any case. By the time concerned citizens begin to see signs of starvation among local deer, most of those deer have already gone through changes that predispose them to disaster. Given the chance, starving deer will gorge themselves on feed. Their stomachs, however, by that time contain too few rumen bacteria to ferment the sudden abundance of plant matter. The deer bloat up and die. Often deer mortality peaks well after emergency feeding began—the deer die not of starvation but of too much food too suddenly.

Feeding programs work best when deer receive supplemental feed before they begin to starve. The problem remains, however, that allowing too many deer to survive and breed again the following year just adds more deer to an already overcrowded habitat.

Predation—by wolves, cougars, coyotes or human hunters—is Nature's merciful alternative to starvation. Where human prejudice has banished four-legged predators—and where changing social values also banish human hunters—deer populations consistently build up to numbers that damage vegetation and stimulate public demand for compassionate winter feeding programs. Such compassion, however, risks making paupers of wild animals and tattered ruins of natural ecosystems. In the long run, feeding deer is as self-defeating as it is unnatural.

Mule Deer Predation

Coyotes, cougars and humans are the primary mule deer predators throughout most of their range. Coyotes rarely attack adult mule deer, except during severe winters, but can be very efficient fawn predators. Cougars, on the other hand, hunt young and old alike. Humans concentrate on mature bucks or, where high deer numbers result in special hunting regulations, adult does.

Mule deer cope with predators by spending a lot of time in open country, often in small herds. When a predator approaches, the deer usually watch its approach and then flee cross-country or uphill into broken terrain. Startled mule deer often run or stot a short distance and then stop to watch. This behavior serves them well with most predators, but not those armed with long-range firearms. Human hunting has selected increasingly for different behavior— many large mule deer bucks now rarely leave dense hiding cover during daylight.

Unlike whitetails, mule deer have an additional defense against predators: they fight back. Solitary dogs or coyotes can rarely stand against the determined mobbing of a group of does; any that are foolish enough to try can suffer serious injuries from sharp hooves.

Predators—especially coyotes and wolves—help keep mule deer herds healthy by constantly detecting and killing weak individuals. It is probably no accident that chronic wasting syndrome has never been found where mule deer coexist with wolves or unhunted coyote populations. The main effect of mountain lions, however, is probably to keep mule deer alert and well dispersed. Severe winters and, in the southern parts of their range, bad droughts probably kill far more deer than most predators. Even so, predators help limit the growth of deer herds and, consequently, reduce damage to habitat from overgrazing.

Mule Deer Decline

After the losses of the 19th century, it looked like the tide had turned in the 20th century. Mule deer numbers increased across the West until, by the 1950s and 1960s, the

Forest dying out from too much browsing

Don't Shoot the Decoy!

Poachers prefer to shoot deer when the odds of getting caught are poorest and the odds of finding deer are greatest. That's why many prefer jack lighting. Driving slowly along the edges of farm fields late at night, these poachers periodically sweep the field with powerful spotlights. If they detect the telltale glow of deer eyes, they hold the deer transfixed in the powerful beam and shoot it with a powerful rifle. If the deer does not fall in its tracks, there is a good chance they will never find it in the darkness beyond the spotlight beam. But the rotting carcass in the woods is no bother -- poachers don't worry about limits. They just go shoot another deer.

Game wardens work hard to deter jack lighting poachers because of the waste of game and the danger from bullets flying randomly into the darkness. One of the most effective tools in the game warden's arsenal is the dummy deer, complete with glow-in-the-dark eyes. Wardens post a lifelike, full-sized deer in a choice location, then hide nearby, watching and videotaping each vehicle that passes.

Some poachers know the deer is a dummy and shout insults at the hidden officers. Others, however, stop and open fire. More than once, poachers have continued firing long after it should have been obvious the deer wasn't real. One excited poacher even ran up and tried to push a dummy deer over.

As wildlife agencies across the west have adopted dummy deer, night poaching has become a chancier business. Seasoned poachers have become dummy-shy, forcing game wardens to become increasingly sophisticated. Some dummy systems now have remote-controlled movable heads, or extra eye sets that flash on and off deeper in the woods to seem like a herd of deer.

Mule deer leaping

region seemed virtually overrun with mule deer. A generation of hikers, deer hunters and naturalists grew up surrounded with deer and convinced that this was the normal situation.

But in the 1970s mule deer populations began to shrink. The decline continues today. The fact that the decline seems to be happening everywhere in the West, combined with the economic importance of deer hunting and the value many people place on abundant deer populations, has resulted in growing concern. Some people blame habitat deterioration because of heavy livestock grazing and lack of wildfire. Others wonder if disease is a factor. Inevitably, many hunters and ranchers blame predators. Others blame overhunting. The common theme in most discussions about mule deer decline is that it is someone else's fault.

Jim Posewitz is an exception. He retired from a 32-year career with the Montana Department of Fish, Wildlife and Parks and became a founding member of Orion, The Hunting Institute. Like most biologists Mr. Posewitz thinks mule deer have decreased because of a variety of factors, but he mostly blames hidebound state wildlife agencies like the one where he once worked.

"I think it was mostly a case of mismanagement, the kind of thing that happens when management agencies are too slow or incapable of responding to changing conditions. Val Geist blames the loss of older-age males through open buck seasons, because the older bucks control the breeding. But state agencies will never acknowledge that behavior is part of biology. Most states still allow hunting right through the Thanksgiving weekend, when bucks are very vulnerable because of the rut. Predation is a factor too—cougar numbers are at high levels and there's a more chaotic lion society because

most mountain lions are killed by hunters with outfitters. They kill mostly the old males that are the ones that would otherwise be controlling things by killing or driving off the younger lions. So, with deer populations already suffering from mismanagement of hunting seasons, the damaged habitat and high predator numbers can keep them down."

Predators are easy scapegoats for any hunter looking at reduced deer numbers. Colorado game warden Jim Haskins, nonetheless, suspects that predators have played a role in mule deer decline—because widespread poisoning campaigns kept coyote and cougar populations unnaturally low in the 1960s and 1970s. "I really think if you look back to the deer we had in the 60s and 70s it probably was an artifact of predator control—and we probably had too many deer."

Haskins and his colleagues agree with Posewitz that mule deer numbers may be dropping because of poorly designed hunting seasons. They point out that when too many hunters harass or shoot buck mule deer during their November breeding season, many does miss the opportunity to breed. If that happens, they come into heat again a month later. If a buck fails to breed them then, they wait another month and come into heat yet again. Does bred later give birth later—and coyotes get two or more chances to hunt newborn fawns rather than just one. One southern Colorado wildlife manager explains, "So without changing the actual number of predators you've changed the effectiveness of predators. Predators can have a bigger impact simply because of our hunting regulations. On top of that, when we come into the winter with younger fawns, that makes them more vulnerable if we have a hard winter."

Others point out that while mule deer numbers drop, elk are increasing. Elk can switch readily from grazing on dry grasses—which mule deer avoid—to eating twigs, leaf buds and other deer foods. Elk, having larger bodies, also have more energy reserves to help them through periods of winter scarcity.

Mule deer may have trouble competing with their larger relatives.

Whatever the causes of mule deer decline, the solution will have to be complex. Most wildlife biologists call for habitat restoration through prescribed fire, hunting regulation changes to keep more bucks alive and reduce hunting pressure during the rut,

and more effective control of elk numbers in some critical areas.

Chronic Wasting Disease

Similar to mad cow disease, this ailment was unknown in wild ungulates until research facilities and deer farms began to concentrate deer and elk in close quarters. Now it is spreading from game farms into wild populations. Wildlife authorities are more than a little uneasy over the potential consequences.

Chronic wasting disease (CWD)apparently made its North American debut at a research center in Fort Collins, Colorado, where it appeared in captive deer in 1967. Like brucellosis and other diseases, it spread from domestic animals into the wild—biologists estimate 10 to 15 percent of some mule deer herds in northeastern and north central Colorado and southeastern Wyoming are infected. Captive elk imported from a South Dakota game farm carried the disease into Canada in 1989. In 1999, CWD turned up for the first time in Montana again, in game farms. Wildlife authorities learned in 2000, to their horror, that the disease had jumped from Saskatchewan game farms into wild deer herds.

Animals afflicted with chronic wasting syndrome appear listless and unconcerned with danger. They lose weight, salivate and urinate excessively, and inevitably die.

The prion—a simple protein fragment unlike either a virus or bacteria—that transmits the disease resists both

heat and drying. Most biologists advise people to avoid any contact with brain, nerve material or bone marrow from wild ungulates that may be affected. If, as some suspect, CWD is simply a variant of mad cow disease transmitted to wildlife, the risk of infection is a serious concern. Because CWD is very similar to mad coe disease, public health experts worry that humans may contract the disease. In ritain more than a hundred people have died after eating beef products from infected animals.

Antlered ungulates commonly chew on old bones, including those of domestic sheep that have died of scapies, a domestic version of chronic wasting disease. Horned ungulates such as pronghorn, bighorn sheep and bison, on the other hand, never chew bones. The fact that chronic wasting disease so far has shown up only in deer and elk leads many biologists to believe that bone-chewing plays a role in the spread of this disease.

A young Utah hunter contracted Creutzfeld-Jakob Disease (terminal dementia) in 1998. Although authorities insisted he had developed the disease from other causes, wildlife biologists felt chills running down their spines. The risk has the Colorado Division of Wildlife pondering the ethics of continuing to allow hunting of deer and elk herds known to be infected.

Mad cow disease resulted from keeping cattle in crowded conditions and feeding them with products derived from carcasses, includ-

Mulie

ing brains, of other livestock. Wild deer and elk live under very different conditions. Chronic wasting disease will likely remain relatively scarce in wild herds—especially as wolves repopulate the west and again take up their age-old role of killing sick creatures.

Living with Mule Deer

Through most of the West, mule deer summer in high mountains and migrate down to winter in low elevation valleys where the climate is mild. Ranchers have used those valleys for generations as their home bases. More recently, lifestyle migrants have subdivided the valley lands for rural acreages and resorts. The interests of mule deer and humans come into conflict when too many people want to take

over deer habitat. In the emerging "New West"—a cluttered sort of place full of permanent human residents who want to feel native to the scenic places they have appropriated—those conflicts will have to find resolution if mule deer are to persist.

Agriculture

Mule deer thrive on alfalfa, both growing and cured. Herds of 50 to 100 mule deer are a common sight on fields of cultivated hay that contain alfalfa or other domestic legumes. Although mule deer grazing puts growing forage plants under stress, few ranchers or farmers begrudge them their meals—as long as state and provincial wildlife agencies issue enough hunting licenses to dampen the growth of the herds. Deer in grain and vegetable fields, however, can

become a serious problem. In chronic problem areas farmers often resort to putting out scarecrows or even automatic-firing scare guns.

Most ranchland conflicts with mule deer happen when large herds of hungry deer congregate on winter ranges. Especially when snow is deep deer find stored hay bales irresistible. Deer climb onto haystacks and pull them apart, urinating and defecating on the hay as they feed. The damaged hay can become unusable for livestock feeding—a serious problem for a rancher whose entire livelihood depends on keeping his stock well fed and healthy through the winter.

Where depredation problems persist, wildlife agencies sometimes respond by selling extra doe hunting permits to reduce the deer populations. They sometimes schedule extended hunting seasons to harass the herds that feed on stored hay. In some western states and provinces, wildlife officials offer ranchers subsidized or free fencing material so that they can enclose their stack yards in eight-foot-high, deer-proof fences. Most farmers and ranchers appreciate having mule deer around and are happy to share some of their crops with wildlife—their main concern is to have some way of responding to problems when those develop.

White-tailed Deer
(Odocoileus virginianus)

Whitetails raise their flag-like tail when startled

Big-eyed, sleek and nervous, the whitetail is the living expression of grace. Thousands of years of forest life have produced an animal of hair-trigger alertness, capable of springing over a seven-foot-high fence, running 60 km/h (37 mph) and bounding more than 20 feet horizontally. The most prolific of our native deer, the whitetail is the product of generations of contact with wild hunters—an elegant, fine-tuned, powerful survivor.

The secretive, forest-dwelling nature of the whitetail served it well as human settlement spread across North America. While most of its predators have vanished and other ungulates have had to retreat to patches of lightly-peopled habitat, whitetails have thrived and increased. Early naturalists considered whitetails rare or nonexistent in prairie Canada and most of the Pacific Northwest. The little deer are abundant there today. Almost exterminated in the eastern states and provinces, whitetails may be as common now as ever before in history. Many habitat changes resulting from forestry and agriculture have produced good deer habitat where once there was none.

Whitetails thrive amid human settlement because they are small, largely nocturnal, and adapted to make a living in patchwork habitats well-populated with predators—including humans. Their long association with humans is evident from archaeological remains all across the continent. Antlers and bones formed a variety of tools, including scrapers, awls, carving and digging implements and ceremonial items. Because white-tailed deer were the most widespread and accessible large prey across most of eastern North America their hides provided clothing and their meat was valued food. Deer hides became buckskin by way of a careful process: scraping the fat and sinew from the hide; removing the hair; rubbing grease into the hide and treating it with crushed brain or liver; soaking it in water; and then chewing it or tenderizing it mechanically with stone or wood implements.

The Sioux were woodland people before moving west onto the Great Plains; in their language the word for white-tailed deer translates to "real meat"—evidence of the important role deer played in their indigenous culture.

Deer benefited from frontier settlement that opened up their forest habitats and provided more food diversity, but massive overhunting more than offset any gains. Almost every pioneer family lived on deer meat, and both pioneers and aboriginal peoples hunted whitetails to supply the lucrative market for deer hides and meat in eastern cities.

Hunters didn't even need licenses to shoot deer until 1864 when New England brought in the first license law. After the 1900 Lacey Act banned interstate trade in wildlife and most states and provinces put closed seasons and bag limits in place, white-tail populations recovered.

Whitetail doe

White-tailed Deer Facts

Length:
bucks: 100-200 cm. (3.2-6.4 ft.)
does: 75-150 cm. (2.5-5 ft.)
Weight:
bucks: 75-190 kg. (165-415 lbs.)
does: 30-100 kg. (65-220 lbs)
Description:
Reddish-brown in summer; grey in winter. White band around the nose and white eye markings. Brown tail with white underside; when startled it raises its tail over its back like a flag, exposing the white underside. Fawns are orange-brown with white spots. Bucks have antlers that sweep forward over the face with each point (tine) emerging from the top. Whitetails gallop and bound when running.
Life Span:
Up to 20 years; most deer, however, live less than ten years.
Reproduction:
First breed at seven months old on good range; otherwise at a year old. Twin fawns are usual; about ten to fifteen out of every hundred does give birth to triplets. Yearling does and does on poor range may produce single fawns.
Food:
Forbs and leaves in summer; fallen leaves, buds and evergreen plants in winter.
Distribution:
Eastern North America north to the edges of the boreal forest from Quebec west to Alberta. Southward, whitetails range through Mexico into Central America. They range throughout the lower valleys of the northern Rockies from B.C. south to Idaho and Wyoming, but are limited to eastern Colorado and New Mexico. Coues whitetail, a small race, lives in southern Arizona and New Mexico.

White-tailed Deer Habitat

River bottom forests, irrigated farmland and deciduous lowlands are home to western whitetails. Unlike mule deer, whitetails are rarely migratory. Some, in fact, live out their entire lives within the same one or two square mile home range. Rich feeding grounds close to good hiding cover are all a whitetail asks of life. Places near water best provide those needs, so whitetails are usually associated with riparian habitats.

Ernest Thompson Seton, in his 1909 *Life-histories of Northern Animals*, said that the whitetail is "...essentially a creature of the denser woods and thickets where these alternate with open glades. Bare plains and rugged hillsides are an abomination unto it; but every Western river whose long flood-flat is belted and patched with far-reaching scrubby thicket is sure to carry with it a long-drawn-out population of skulking Whitetails, which, between scrub and bog, are able to hold their own and multiply, in spite of rifle and Wolf; while the hill-frequenting Blacktail [mule deer] is rapidly passing away."

Where hunting pressure makes life too difficult for mule deer, whitetails can take over their habitat. In Alberta's hunter-crowded Porcupine Hills and some parts of Montana, whitetails have become common in Douglas fir and limber pine forests that crown the high ridges.

Deer avoid direct sunlight on hot days and move from one bedding location to another to remain in the shade. In winter and on cold nights, they bed in warm sites, avoiding frost pockets or wind exposure and often selecting mid-slope locations. In severe winter weather deer put their need for food second to their preference for habitats where they can shelter from wind and deep snow. Eastern whitetails often move into dense conifer thickets where interlaced branches intercept snow that would otherwise bog the deer down. Those same branches, however, also block sunlight. The yarded deer find little useful forage beneath the shady canopy. Some deer yards develop trench-like trails connecting coniferous cover with nearby shrubbery and

Poetry in Motion

Bounding whitetail

"**Of all our deer** the Virginia Deer is decidedly the most beautiful in form as well as graceful in motion. Whether standing quietly on the bank of a streamlet, or bounding through the forest, it equally challenges our admiration. It is the very embodiment of graceful form and agile motion...

"When startled by surprise, the Virginia Deer's first gait is a canter, which it pursues for two, three, or four jumps, when it makes a high, long leap, as if to enable itself to take a broader survey of surrounding objects; then follow a few of the ordinary lower and shorter jumps, which are again succeeded by the high, long leaps, and so on till it becomes satisfied that its apprehensions are groundless, when it subsides to a trot or amble, and then stops, with head and ears erect, and looks with great earnestness at the object which startled it."

John Caton, 1877
The Antelope and Deer of America

Whitetail fawn

hardwood thickets.

Since deer need a mix of food and cover, patchwork landscapes usually offer the best habitat. Where protection from fire, farm windbreaks and ribbons of shrubbery along irrigation ditches have extended woodland cover into open prairie habitats, whitetails have responded by expanding their range into what was formerly forage-rich but cover-poor country. Logging and agricultural clearing along the edges of northern boreal forests also has improved whitetail habitat in what used to be cover-rich but forage-poor country.

Deer have discriminating palates when it comes to green matter. Faced with a great variety of forage choices, deer pick the plants that offer the best combination of starches, protein and trace minerals at any time. They don't just choose between kinds of plants either; they choose the best stands of any given species. When researchers in New York fertilized an oak woodland with nitrogen, deer responded by browsing more than 80 percent of the dogwood shrubs in that stand. Right next door, in unfertilized oak woodland, they browsed only 4 percent of the dogwoods. Deer select clover leaves out of rank suburban lawns, green leaves amid the changing foliage of autumn, and juniper branches with few aromatic oils over adjacent branches with higher amounts.

Whitetail Deer Family Life

Whitetail does give birth in early June when vegetation is lush enough to hide the newborn fawns. Deer in good habitat usually give birth to twins, especially if the previous winter was not too stressful. Triplets are rare, but more common in whitetails than other deer. Yearling does, or does suffering from poor nutrition or too stressful a winter, may only have a single fawn. Fawns born to unhealthy does often die within the first few hours.

When her fawns are born, a doe cleans them thoroughly, eats the afterbirth and licks their rumps to encourage them to void. Her scrupulous care produces two important results—it builds a strong maternal bond to the fawn, and it

Deer Shields

Frontiersmen often used deerskins as armor against Indian arrowheads, shaping the skin and then letting it dry hard rather than tanning it properly.

eliminates odors that might attract predators.

As with other deer, newborn fawns spend most of their first few days lying flat on the ground, perfectly still. They pick a new hiding place each time they nurse. A mother returning to nurse her fawn issues a low-pitched grunt that the fawn responds to with a mew. A frightened fawn or one searching for its mother gives a lamb-like bleat.

Fawns have little odor during the first week of life. Dogs and other predators often pass close by without detecting any hint of their presence. If the doe is near her hidden fawn when a predator approaches, she will often stamp her feet and try to decoy the animal away. Although the mobbing instinct in whitetails is weaker than in mule deer, a doe will sometimes attack a predator to protect her fawn. Dr. David

Mech describes one incident: "...Suddenly the deer rushed the wolf and hit her with both front feet. This bowled over the wolf. The wolf arose again immediately, and the deer charged again and chased the wolf about 25 feet. Three times the deer charged the wolf..." In this instance, the wolf apparently gave up and left, as Mech found no sign of a kill when he returned later.

Within a few days of birth, fawns begin to follow their mothers from one patch of cover to another. They can become quite playful, leaping and bounding or racing away from their mother and then back. By the time the fawns are three weeks old they are fully mobile and remarkably strong. Does and fawns may join other family groups or remain by themselves throughout the summer.

One Buck

In 1784, settlers in what is now Tennessee decided that they should incorporate and establish a government. The short-lived State of Franklin was cash-poor, however, so it paid its civic officials in animal hides. The annual salary of the Governor was 1,000 deerskins. The Chief Justice received 500 deerskins. The system didn't work well and soon broke down because of counterfeiting: lesser officials who were to be paid in raccoon skins complained of getting opossum skins with raccoon tails stitched on. This early attempt at indigenous government, however, had one lasting result: we still call the dollar a "buck."

History's Winner

"Of all the large game of the United States, the white-tail deer is the best known and the most widely distributed...And it is the only ruminant animal which is able to live on in the land even when it has been pretty thickly settled. There is hardly a State wherein it does not still exist, at least in some out-of-the-way corner; and long after the elk and the buffalo have passed away, and when the big-horn and prong-horn have become rare indeed, the white-tail deer will still be common in certain parts of the country."

Theodore Roosevelt, 1885: *Hunting Trips of a Ranchman*

Whitetail Deer Social Life

Like other ungulates, whitetails live in a complex society. Deer compete for social status and enforce it with various physical behaviors. A herd of deer, seemingly concerned only with grazing in a quiet evening meadow, in fact communicate constantly by the way they position their bodies, the angle of their ears and how they approach one another.

Dominant deer are usually older does or bucks. Their large body size and confidence help enforce their superior status. Other deer, by following and submitting to dominant deer, benefit from their greater experience in finding food, shelter and safety. Even so, less influential deer regularly challenge their superiors and, occasionally, succeed in moving up the social ladder. Does chase one another or kick out with their forelegs to assert themselves. Bucks have an additional way of establishing status: they frequently lock antlers with herd-mates and push one another around, testing each other's strength. These sparring matches are more like ritual play than fighting, but they help in setting up a social hierarchy before the breeding season begins.

Bucks and does spend little time together after becoming sexually mature. Bucks remain alone or in small bachelor groups most of the year. Does frequently associate with other does and their fawns, especially in fall and winter when small herds sometimes aggregate into large herds. Whitetail herds are more the product of necessity than choice, however. When deep snow doesn't force them together, whitetails prefer groups of no more than 10 or so.

Bucks spend the spring and summer establishing relationships with other bucks and sorting out dominance. As the nights lengthen and testosterone levels increase, bucks become less tolerant of one another and increasingly interested in does. During the peak of the whitetail rut bucks become obsessed with breed-

ing and travel almost constantly, seeking the sweet scent of does in estrous. In Banff National Park, wardens report that more whitetail bucks die in collisions with automobiles in November than any other month.

White-tailed deer, like mule deer, do not gather harems. Instead, a buck will single out a receptive doe, mate with her over the course of a few hours, and then strike out in search of another doe.

Whitetail Deer Predation

Wolf biologist Dave Mech considers the contest between whitetails and wolves evenly balanced. Whitetails depend on constant vigilance to detect predators before they get too close. Deer run faster than wolves—up to 56 km/h (35 mph)—and deep snow hinders them less, since whitetails bound above the snow while wolves remain closer to the ground where they encounter

Short Days, Long Nights

Deer rut in December or January in Texas and Arizona. In Alberta and British Columbia, however, the whitetail rut is usually about the middle of November. It all has to do with how long the nights are.

Like humans and most other mammals, deer have a pineal gland on the top of their heads, above the eyes. The pineal gland manufactures a hormone called melatonin in response to light. In

fall, days become shorter and nights longer and the amount of melatonin in a deer's body changes. That in turn triggers changes in output of other glands, including sex hormones like testosterone, estrogen and progesterone. Since winter nights grow longer first in the north, northern whitetails go into rut earliest. Southern deer must wait until the middle of winter before the nights are long enough to

trigger rutting behavior. Changes in light levels also influence antler development—antlers sprout when nights are shortest, and continue to grow as lengthening nights increase the buck's testosterone levels.

Scientists have tested this response by removing pineal glands from deer and observing the resultant disruption in their breeding cycles and antler growth.

Making Scents

Subtle messages swirl upon the woodland breezes. Unknowable by humans, whose sense of smell is woefully underdeveloped, the odors which fill deer country are endless sources of important information to deer and other animals. Their highly-developed ability to discriminate among scents helps deer select the best food plants, detect predators, and communicate with one another.

Inter-deer communication depends partly on special glands. These include the tarsals (inside each hind leg right at the hock),

metatarsals (on the outside of each hind leg halfway to the hoof) and interdigitals (between the toes of each foot). Deer leave scent in their tracks from the interdigitals; other deer then know who has been down which trail, and how recently. Deer concentrate their scented signatures by urinating on their hind legs, often rubbing the tarsals together at the same time. If other deer are nearby, they will often sniff them while they are doing it. In doe-fawn herds, fawns appear to use this scent to identify their mothers.

Rutting bucks take great interest in doe urine since its chemical composition indicates whether she is ready to breed. A large, dominant whitetail buck will urinate on his legs, then paw the ground at a trail intersection or in moist soil along a wooded deer trail. When a doe is ready to mate, she may urinate in the buck's scrape, leaving an invitation to follow her scented footsteps and enjoy a brief woodland rendezvous. These rutting scrapes are characteristic of whitetails, but very rarely seen among mule deer.

we could exterminate the Gray-wolf we should half solve the question of deer-supply..." He cited anecdotal accounts of wolves running deer mercilessly until they dropped. In truth, wolves and coyotes rarely chase a deer far before either capturing it or breaking off the chase and looking for easier prey. Well-fed domestic dogs, on the other hand, sometimes chase deer for miles.

Cougars and bobcats are even less likely to try to run a deer down. If a surprise attack fails, the whitetail can usually relax again after a short dash.

Humans hunt deer by a variety of techniques. Unlike other predators that rely on scent and sound to find deer, humans rely almost exclusively on eyesight. Whitetails avoid humans by remaining invisible. In heavily hunted areas, deer often lie flat on the ground like fawns while hunters walk past. They may also crouch or remain stationary in dense brush, or sneak carefully around the sound of an approaching hunter.

Startled, whitetails respond to all predators the same— they sprint rapidly into cover with long, plunging bounds that leave a broken scent trail. Only when securely out of sight and safe from any initial pursuit will a whitetail stand to watch and listen. Then it retreats carefully into dense brush or circles around to check whatever frightened it. Like other ungulates pursued closely by wolves, coyotes or dogs, whitetails commonly bolt downhill for the protection of water.

Cougars rely on surprise-attacks to capture a deer

more friction. Wolves gain the advantage only during brief periods when a heavy crust builds on snow, since a wolf is lighter than a deer relative to the size of its foot.

Ernest Thompson Seton, like most early 20th century naturalists concerned about wildlife scarcity, felt that, "if

Deer and Dogs

Dogs descended from wolves. The impulse to hunt and kill is part of their nature, from the biggest Newfoundland to the tiniest Chihuahua. Indeed, the friendliness, intelligence and learning ability we value so highly in our family pets and herding dogs are wolf traits. So it should come as no surprise when dogs show an instinctive interest in chasing deer.

Unlike wolves, however, most dogs are well fed and have energy to spare. Wolves can't afford to exhaust themselves pursuing hard-to-catch prey. Dogs, on the other hand, often lack the sense to break off pursuit and need not worry about the consequences—there's a bowl of fortified dog food waiting back home. Consequently, loose dogs can be disastrous in deer country. Dogs will run deer to exhaustion. Even if they fail to kill or wound their quarry, many deer succumb later to stress or severe weather. Does may lose their unborn fawns.

Living in deer country is a rare privilege that comes with serious responsibilities. Among those is the obligation to keep all dogs from wandering free, especially at night.

Big Antlers: Where and Why?

Big trophy antlers -- the kind that score high in the Boone and Crockett record book -- are a Holy Grail to some hunters. Hunting magazines compile statistics on counties or regions that produce the greatest number of large-antlered deer. Trophy hunters scour the woodlands in spring, looking for large shed antlers that might betray the local residence of a trophy-class buck.

Big antlers are the product of genetics, forage quality and age. The largest antlers in any deer herd, according to Val Geist, grow on the heads of bucks that abstain from breeding. Heavily hunted deer populations rarely produce trophy-sized bucks because few bucks ever live past their second or third season. Where poor soils produce vegetation that lacks trace minerals, calcium or phosphorus, shortage of raw materials results in smaller antlers than would be the case otherwise.

Trophy hunters distinguish between typical antlers, which are relatively symmetrical and well-formed, and non-typical antlers which may be contorted and bizarre looking. Non-typical antlers can result from injuries a buck suffered while the antlers were growing. Some regions consistently produce non-typical bucks, probably because of genetic features passed on from deer to deer.

Serious big-buck hunters can spend tens of thousands of dollars each year on research and scouting trips. Many are secretive, almost paranoid individuals who guard their secrets jealously. Some resort to unethical or even illegal tactics to get the deer they want.

Even so, many of the largest bucks in the record books fell to average hunters who just happened to be lucky. The largest typical buck in the world was shot on November 23, 1993, by Milo Hansen on his farm near Biggar, Saskatchewan. Scoring 213 1/8 Boone and Crockett points, it replaced the "Jordan Buck," shot in the eastern U.S. 80 years previously.

Whitetail buck

Living with Whitetail Deer

Whitetails adapt quickly to protection. Where humans no longer hunt them, deer often move into town. There they learn to treat people as little more than scenery. Sometimes, in fact, whitetails become aggressive.

Because deer are attractive, appealing animals, many people become fiercely protective of their local herds. Some rural acreage owners even buy feed for wintering deer to attract them closer to their homes.

Artificial feeding and protection from hunting, along with reduced populations of other predatory animals in built-up areas, commonly result in deer population explosions. Whitetails, after all, are prolific by design. Overproduction of young compensates for high losses to predators. Without predation deer numbers increase—and so does damage to gardens, ornamentals and wild vegetation. If the herds have access to farmland or orchards, agricultural crops face increased depredations. The protected deer become heavy and placid.

Heavily populated rural areas normally have high road densities and lots of traffic. Automobiles take over some of the herd-thinning role that starvation and predators would otherwise play. However, roadkills damage cars and sometimes injure or kill humans too. Some counties promote special shotgun or archery hunts to reduce deer herds. These are usually ineffective, however, since many property owners deny hunters access and deer are quick to recognize places of safe refuge.

Highway authorities try to reduce collisions with deer by installing special headlight reflectors that shine into deer eyes when cars approach. At low traffic volumes this can help by making the deer freeze temporarily until the automobile passes. High-volume roads, however, inevitably kill deer. High fences can keep deer off roads, and bridges or culvert underpasses can help deer get across the rights of way without having to dash between cars, but these are expensive measures. Most highway authorities only reluctantly spend money on wildlife safety.

Some drivers purchase fixtures for their vehicles that produce a high-pitched sound as wind rushes through them. Field studies of these devices show that deer do hear the sound and, at least in some areas, roadkills may decline. Controlled studies at Texas A&M University, however, suggest that the devices are usually ineffective.

Even where annual hunting reduces deer numbers, roadkills are a problem where roads and vehicles are abundant. Knowledgeable drivers slow down at dusk and dawn and watch for eyeshine in road ditches. If they spot deer near the road, they turn on emergency flashers or flicker their headlights to alert other drivers. They know that deer often watch approaching cars—only to dash onto the road at the last minute, when least expected.

Deer Hunting

Opening day of deer season is a cultural tradition as endemic to North America as Thanksgiving or Mother's day. Lights appear in kitchen windows long before dawn. Headlights snake out of towns and cities as the first faint glow of daybreak appears along the eastern skyline. Teenage hunters, tense with anticipation, peer intently out windows into shadowed fields, hoping to spot a deer. Older hunters talk quietly about past hunts or today's strategy, looking forward to immersing themselves again in the sounds, smells and sensations of the autumn woods.

The first gunshot breaks the predawn stillness before color has begun to tint the pale outlines of the awakening world. Farmers and their families listen with conflicting emotions as the sound of gunshots swells. They're glad the hunting season will reduce the number of deer closer to what the landscape can sustain, but it feels uncomfortable to have so many armed strangers out there. Every year bullets pass dangerously close to houses and school buses.

Non hunters passing by on their way to work or school glimpse the distinctive garb of hunters and wonder how anyone could deliberately shoot

Southern Cross

When game farmers transplanted North American deer to New Zealand, in the Southern Hemisphere, the deer began to rut about six months earlier because the seasons are reversed south of the equator—July has the longest nights and January the shortest.

White-tailed deer bucks

The Price of Protection

Researchers from the Universities of New York and Minneapolis have shown that too many deer in too small an area can devastate rare plants. They studied three deer herds in isolated patches of Minnesota's once vast "Big Woods." Two populations received protection from hunters; the third did not. In the two protected areas, white-tailed deer ate 75 percent of the white trilliums that carpet the forest floor each spring. Where hunting was permitted -- and deer numbers consequently lower—most trilliums flowered and set seed without getting nipped by deer. The researchers concluded that in the badly fragmented remains of many eastern ecosystems—where few deer predators survive—deer can drive palatable plants extinct.

Biologist Thomas Rooney studied the Heart's Content Forest in Pennsylvania—one of the last unlogged stands of the region's original forests. He compared the modern flora to a list of plants recorded in the same forest 70 years earlier. Between 60-80 percent had vanished—mostly because of unnaturally high deer populations. Even trees such as the eastern hemlock suffer from deer browsing. According to botanist Dan Waller of the University of Wisconsin, vulnerable native plants are disappearing from eastern forests because of deer herds twice to four times more dense than when Europeans first settled the region. He blames wildlife agencies that maintain the highest possible numbers of deer for hunters. The time has come, he argues, to put hunters to work reducing the size of those herds so the depleted forests can heal.

He gets no argument from Ontario environmentalist Mary Gartshore. She works to restore the rich Carolinian forest ecosystem that once spread along the Niagara Peninsula and the north shore of Lake Erie. One of her goals as a conservation activist is to make people aware of the threatened beauty of the last forest fragments. "After some of my talks people ask me what they can do to help restore the Carolinian forest," she says. "I tell them: eat more venison."

an animal so graceful and harmless as a deer. To them, the hunters are almost alien. The camouflage or bright orange clothing and shoulder-slung rifles are disturbing and dangerous looking.

Down in the woods, those hunters watch deer trails or the edge of farm fields, hoping to intercept a deer on its way from feeding areas to bedding cover. Others sneak slowly through the forest, placing each step carefully and watching closely for the faintest flicker of movement that might betray prey. Some parties of hunters organize drives, with some posted at likely escape routes while the rest walk noisily abreast, trying to scare

deer out ahead of them.

If snow has fallen, solitary hunters may follow tracks in hopes of overtaking a deer and seeing it before it spots them. Chickadees scold. The breeze is pungent with rotting leaves. The workaday world is forgotten; everything is the hunt.

Most modern hunting techniques are variations on those practiced by countless generations of aboriginal North Americans. Only the trappings of the hunt have changed—highly accurate firearms and compound bows have replaced straight bows and spears, buckskin has given way to synthetic fleece and fibers, and hunters travel to and from their chosen haunts

by motor vehicle rather than afoot. To the deer, however, these are familiar predators—and, on average, easier to avoid than they used to be.

Some modern hunting techniques, however, tilt the balance in favor of the hunter. Some hunters use diaphragm calls that let them mimic the call of a lost fawn, an amorous doe or an excited buck. Chemical scents hide human odors and, in some cases, attract deer. A few obsessive types use trip wires, hidden cameras or other remote sensing devices to betray the movement patterns of their intended prey. A growing minority even shoots deer from tree stands over bait—grain, rotten apples or molasses. Shooting deer over bait, however, is not hunting. Real hunters consider the practice corrupt - exploiting a deer's inability to resist high-quality food demands neither skill nor honor.

The urge some hunters feel to kill large trophy deer drives most unethical hunting practises and turns some into poachers. It's an age-old urge. Serious hunters, however, know they must temper that urge with ethical restraint and determined respect for the animals they hunt. Trophy hunting at its best gives a hunter the chance to hone his or her woodcraft skills while leaving most deer undisturbed. Some trophy hunters will go for years before killing an animal, while those of us who hunt for meat take prey home almost every year.

Deer Farming

The first director of the New York Zoological Society, William Hornaday, became an anti-hunter, and a pro game rancher, both for the same reason: his panic over what he saw in the early 1900s as the impending loss of North American wildlife. His prescription for conservation of large ungulates: turn them into agricultural crops.

"As a state and county asset, the white-tailed deer contains possibilities that as yet seem to be ignored by the American people as a whole. It is quite time to consider that persistent, prolific and toothsome animal... Every year the people of the United States are wasting uncountable millions of pounds of venison, because we are neglecting our opportunities for producing it practically without cost. Imagine for a moment bestowing upon land owners the

ability to stock with white-tailed and Indian sambar deer all the wild lands of the United States that are suitable for those species..."

Largely dismissed at the time, his ideas seem belatedly to have come of age in the 1990s -- much to the horror of those who value wild animals and natural habitat.

Today, of course, white-tailed deer numbers have rebounded largely because of their management as game animals -- public resources -- not in spite of it. To those who value North America's 20th century tradition of public wildlife management, enclosing deer behind farm fences is not the panacea Hornaday proposed. They see it as the beginning of the end for a system of conservation that Hornaday never imagined -- one that works.

Moose *(Alces alces)*

Cow moose

All legs and nose—dark, somber and massive—moose look like holdovers from the Pleistocene. The largest antlered animal in North America—second only to the bison as the continent's largest land mammal—moose can weigh more than half a ton and stand eight feet high.

Solitary figures of the forest edge, moose trace hidden trails through willow thickets and aspen groves, crashing suddenly away when surprised at close range.

Moose are northern ungulates who range across northern Europe, Asia and North America wherever spruce, aspen, willow and birch are abundant. In the Rocky Mountains their habitat becomes patchy southwards, petering out altogether in northern Utah and Colorado. They favor colder, snowier country than elk and deer—only the mountain caribou can live under harsher winter conditions than the moose.

The largest moose are in Alaska and Yukon. The subspecies of moose that ranges from extreme southern British Columbia and Alberta south to Colorado and Utah is Shiras' moose—*Alces alces shirasi*—the smallest variety of moose on the continent. Shiras' moose has smaller antlers, a shorter neck and greyer body coloration than more northerly moose. Even so, a fully-grown Shiras' moose is half again as large as an elk the same age.

Moose Habitat

Grass rarely means much to moose. Sedges and other wetland plants, on the other hand, are important summer foods. Most of the year, moose rely on browse for food—young twigs, buds, leaves and other woody material. Where moose are abundant, willows and young poplars often take on a dense, hedged appearance because of heavy browsing. When moose eat the ends of branches, small buds along the sides of the branch sprout and grow. Moose then eat the ends of the new side branches, triggering the growth of still

Left: Bull moose can develop enormous antlers

Moose like wet places

more side branches. The more heavily-browsed a shrub, the shorter each new set of side branches. Eventually, if browsed often enough, a shrub may die because of its inability to replace the living material it loses.

Moose prefer rolling terrain with a mixture of coniferous trees—spruce, pine and fir - and deciduous growth—aspen, balsam poplar, willow and birch. The conifers protect moose from wind and cold, as well as intercepting winter snow in their canopies. The deciduous trees and shrubs are food. If the landscape is poorly drained and ribboned with small streams, so much the better because moose, more than any other ungulates, like wet places. In summer, in fact, moose often feed on pondweeds and other underwater vegetation. Moose even dive completely under-

Moose Facts

Length:
bulls: 250-300 cm. (8-10 feet)
cows: 200-275 cm. (6.5-9 feet)
Weight:
bulls: 380-530 kg. (850-1200 lbs.)
cows: 270-360 kg. (600-800 lbs)
Description:
Moose have long legs, a blocky body with a pronounced shoulder hump, ponderous noses, long ears and a "bell" or dewlap hanging from their necks. Most are dark brown, almost black, with whitish hind legs. Moose run with a bouncing trot.
Life Span:
Rarely twenty years. Most moose die before the age of ten.
Reproduction:
First breed at sixteen months of age -- later, under poor habitat conditions. Most cows have a single calf, but about a quarter have twins. Triplets are very rare.
Food:
 Leaves, young twigs and buds of woody plants. In summer, moose add tall forbs, pondweeds and aquatic plants to their diet.
Distribution:
The coniferous forest regions of northern Europe, Asia and North America. In the Rocky Mountains, moose range as far south as northern Utah and Colorado, and have been introduced successfully in good habitat farther south.

Fire and Water

Burnt forest near Jasper, Alberta: rejuvenated ungulate habitat.

Natural disasters are good news from a moose's point of view. Floods and high water create and sustain most core moose ranges, while forest fires produce some of their most productive - although temporary -- habitats. Most moose in the Rocky Mountains live near mountain streams where spring runoff continually rearranges the floodplain, creating a rich mosaic of spruce forest, aspen and poplar groves and dense shrubbery. Complexes of beaverponds are particularly good for moose because of the lush growth of willows.

Moose also like the abundance of green shrubbery that results from another kind of natural disaster. Avalanches regularly scour away the encroaching forest cover from steep mountainsides. In the northern Rockies, moose sometimes winter on avalanche-scarred mountainsides -- evidently preferring the risk of burial to the more frequent encounters with wolves that they could expect if they wintered at lower elevations near rivers.

Wildfire -- which strikes fear into the hearts of most foresters and anyone who owns a cabin or resort -- removes forest cover and opens the forest floor to rain and sun. Moose colonize recently burned areas and can become remarkably abundant for about 30 or 40 years after the fire. When a 450 square mile area in Alaska burned in 1947, aspen trees scattered through the area sprouted from their roots, becoming much more abundant than before the fire. By 1950, 273 moose were wintering in the burn. Only three years later, the count had climbed to 1,111.

Most of the dead trees left standing after a fire eventually fall down, littering the landscape like a jumble of giant jackstraws. Long-legged moose have no difficulty navigating the tangles. Their predators, however, do.

Smoky Bear has done such a good job of promoting fire control, unfortunately, that much of the West is marginal moose habitat today. Wildlife and forest agencies have begun to restore fire to its historic role in shaping the western landscape. Moose populations will almost certainly expand as fires return to the land.

water to pull up greenery from shallow lake bottoms.

Dense forest is nearly as unfriendly to hungry moose as open grasslands. Although a moose can reach up to nine or 10 feet to pull down forage, moose most prefer young forests or patchworks of vegetation where they can find abundant shoulder-height greenery.

Moose Family Life

Few sights are so terrifying as an angry cow moose defending her calf. Moose calves first appear in late May or early June. Cows often give birth on small islands in lakes or rivers, or in dense cover along valley bottoms. They choose isolated sites to avoid bears and other predators who actively hunt the newborns at this season. If a predator—or an unsuspecting hiker—gets too close to a cow's hidden calf, the massive mother can become a dangerous adversary. Cow moose charge predators and attempt to kick them with their front legs.

Military Moose

Moose tolerate swamps and rough terrain better than horses. They have a smooth, ground-covering gait too. So in the early 1700s, military planners in Sweden came up with the idea of mounting their cavalry on moose and sending them into battle. The idea had some merit. Moose proved easy to train and ride. The experiment failed however, since they turned tail and fled whenever the shooting started. Which suggests that moose are smarter than horses.

Like other ungulates, moose calves lie immobile and rely on their small size and relative lack of body odor to protect them from predators until they are a week or two old and strong enough to keep pace with their mothers. Even then, if danger threatens, the calf scoots into dense cover and hides while the mother distracts or attacks the intruder.

Most cow moose have a single calf. One-year-old females can breed and give birth but most wait until their second year, especially where the habitat is relatively poor. Both the age of first breeding and the likelihood of giving birth to more than one calf depend on how well fed and healthy the cow moose is. Rarely do more than a quarter of the cows in a given population give birth to twin calves. Triplets are very rare. Moose generally reproduce more slowly than deer or elk except where fire or logging produce an abundance of high-quality forage.

Calf moose stay with their mothers well into the winter, but the bond rarely lasts into the following spring. The pregnant cow prefers to wander off alone to give birth. Yearling offspring, because of their relatively small size and lack of experience, are vulnerable to

Shiras' Moose

Shiras' moose

George Shiras pioneered flash photography of animals at night. His photos appeared in National Geographic articles between 1912 and 1921. In 1935, the National Geographic Society published his two-volume book Hunting Wild Life with Camera and Flashlight. He explored the area in and around Yellowstone National Park between 1908 and 1910, documenting the presence of a distinctive population of moose in northern Wyoming. In 1914, taxonomist E.W. Wilson described the new subspecies of moose in a scientific paper and named it Shiras' moose in honor of the naturalist-photographer.

predators and accidents until they reach their full growth at about two to four years of age.

Moose Society

Solitude doesn't trouble a moose—in fact, most prefer it. Moose are the least sociable of all North American ungulates. Small groups of three or four bull moose are not uncommon in summer, but cows usually remain alone with their young of the year. The two sexes develop a greater interest in one another after the aspen and poplar trees have yellowed and the forests are beginning to look threadbare. The mid October rut is brief but intense. Bull moose make large scrapes, like whitetail bucks, which they scent mark with urine and odor from glands in their hooves. The bulls issue low-pitched grunts to advertise their presence. Cows also vocalize, with deep mooing sounds or moans. Bull moose thrash shrubs with their antlers or engage in short, noisy sparring matches with other bulls.

Temporary groupings of bull and cow moose during the rut quickly break down once the breeding is done. Moose continue to advertise their presence to one another, mostly by scent, after they have resumed their solitary lives. Most moose in a region know one another and know their own place in the social hierarchy, even though they meet only occasionally.

Southern Moose

Bull moose

It doesn't much matter that the habitat is ideal for moose, if they have no way of getting there. That's probably why moose tracks have never laced the rich beaver meadows and aspen woodlands of Colorado's North Park, Middle Park, Laramie River and upper Rio Grande basin. Open sagebrush parks and other unfriendly terrain separated these islands of potential moose country from southern Wyoming's sparse population of Shiras' moose.

In 1978 the Colorado Division of Wildlife hopscotched moose across that marginal habitat. Biologists captured moose from Wyoming and Montana, trucked them south, and released them in the southern Rockies. The transplant program was a success—today more than 1,000 moose occupy the central and southern part of the state. The introduced population has done so well that a few lottery- selected hunters fill their freezers each fall with some of the best wild ungulate meat in North America. Unfortunately, each fall a few moose also fall to poachers and irresponsible elk hunters who fail to make sure of what kind of animal they were looking at.

Good viewing locations for Colorado moose are riparian willow thickets along the upper Rio Grande River near Creede, and the Illinois River near Rand.

Overleaf: Moose cow with young calf

Moose Through the Seasons

Northern moose are among the least migratory of ungulates but even so, especially in mountainous regions, moose travel regularly between seasonal ranges. One of the main triggers for seasonal migrations is deep snow. In the Rockies, more snow falls at higher elevations than lower down. Moose can remain in the lush feeding grounds near timberline and on high avalanche slopes well into November most years, but as the snow grows deep moose soon find that the energy cost of moving about is more than they can endure. Moose rarely linger long where snow is deeper than 2 1/4 feet (75 cm.).

In British Columbia's Glacier National Park moose sometimes winter in snow five or more feet deep. They take advantage of the hollows beneath large cedar trees to avoid the deepest snow. Hidden crusts in the snowpack can support the weight of a moose through most of the winter. However, snow-country moose can be in poor condition, and seldom produce more than a single calf the following spring. The one advantage they enjoy over moose that winter at lower elevations is safety from predators.

As high country snow levels increase, moose shift to lower elevations or to foothills locations where they can travel more efficiently. Even so, they remain in forests, usually at a higher elevation than elk or deer. Aspen forests become increasingly important as winter progresses and deepening snow chokes wetland hollows. Dry winter browse is poor quality food compared with the soft greenery of sum-

Ticks

Most large ungulates in the Rocky Mountains have to cope with ticks. These small, crawling creatures are related to spiders. They live in tall grass, junipers and shrubbery and cling to exposed surfaces waiting for a passing animal to rub against them. Once aboard their future host, ticks burrow into its hair and travel until they find a warm place in the hollow of a leg, on the neck, behind the ear or elsewhere. There, they lock their mouthparts into the skin and begin to feed on their host's blood. Growing ticks can swell to the size of a grape as their abdominal cavities fill with blood. Magpies often land on the backs of tick-infected elk, bighorn sheep or deer and pick the engorged ticks off.

Ticks are most active in early spring after the snow has first melted off. When Native Americans commonly set fire to favored hunting areas, spring fires doubtless helped keep tick populations down. Today, lacking fire, some parts of the West have substantial tick populations that can heavily infect wild animals.

Any heavy tick infestation reduces the vigor of the host animal and

Rocky Mountain wood tick

makes it vulnerable to other problems. The worst problems develop in places where ungulates are forced to concentrate on small winter ranges. In those situations not only can ticks thrive because of the abundance of host animals but other parasites may already have infected the animals, making them less able to cope with blood loss to ticks.

In parts of Montana, biologists have found young elk that appeared to have died as a direct result of extreme tick infestations.

Ticks readily latch onto human hosts too. This can lead, in some regions, to tick paralysis, Rocky Mountain spotted fever, Lyme's disease or other infections. Removing the tick carefully -- making sure to get the head and mouthparts that often remain attached when someone jerks a tick off them - usually takes care of any potential health risks. However, any bruising, discoloration or flu-like symptoms that set in immediately after exposure to ticks always warrant a visit to the doctor. Tick-related illnesses can be devastating if not treated quickly.

Moose foraging in winter on young branches and buds

The Bull Moose Party

When Theodore Roosevelt parted ways with the Republican Party in 1912, he ran for a third term as president of the United States under the banner of the Bull Moose Party (the Progressives). One of his campaign photos showed the bespectacled conservationist sitting on the back of a moose. The photo was actually a composite of two images; history does not record that Roosevelt ever actually got astride of a living moose.

According to his biographers, however, Roosevelt made good use of his knowledge of moose hunting when the occasion arose unexpectedly on a campaign stop in Milwaukee Wisconsin. Roosevelt was bowing to an audience from a touring car when a would-be assassin shot him in the chest. Roosevelt insisted on continuing on to a speaking engagement in spite of his wound. When he reached into his vest pocket for his speech, however, he found that the bullet had gone through the speech and shattered his metal spectacles case. Roosevelt waved the broken case in the air and said, "It takes more than that to kill a Bull Moose!"

Roosevelt lost the 1912 election, but he never lost the bullet. Doctors advised him that removing it from his chest would be too risky, so it remained there until the stocky ex-president died in 1919.

mer. Wintering moose travel little and spend a lot of time bedded down, especially on sun-exposed slopes, so their energy needs are lower than in summer when cows are nursing calves and bulls are growing new antlers. Dense late winter snow supports the weight of hungry moose, allowing them to reach buds and young branches that were too high for them earlier in the winter.

The first breaking buds and new spring greenery mark the end of months of slow starvation. Warm days and freezing nights convert soft, fluffy snow to a denser, more granular snowpack that can support the weight of moose, and they begin to disperse back into higher elevation wetlands or

Moose with velvet antlers

forests. During the snow-free seasons, moose spend a lot of time in shrubby habitats such as creek bottoms, avalanche slopes and burns, rather than in mature poplar and conifer forests.

Meningeal Brainworm

Snails are slow, harmless-looking creatures, but they can bring down a half-ton moose. "Moose disease" is a lethal condition that inflicts moose at the margins of their North American range. It is caused by the meningeal worm *Parelaphostrongylus tenuis*, a nematode that has a two-pronged life cycle. Part of its life takes place inside a snail. When the snail climbs onto vegetation it deposits nematode cysts where animals like white-tailed deer or moose are most likely to ingest them. Once inside its ungulate host, the brainworm migrates into the nervous system. White-tailed deer seem able to coexist with the brainworm; their bodies somehow isolate the worms and protect the brain from extensive damage. Not so with infected moose. They become increasingly disoriented, then paraplegic, and finally die. Elk also have difficulty surviving brainworm infections.

Biologists speculate that one of the main factors limiting the spread of moose in North America is the abundance of white-tailed deer in deciduous forest regions. Whitetails and snails together sustain meningeal brainworm populations, keeping moose confined to regions where whitetails are scarce. As log-

Good Food

Jesuit Nicolas Point said that the Flathead, Couer D'Alene and Blackfoot Indians felt that moose,"...in the quality of its meat, is almost the equal of buffalo." Fur trade explorer David Thompson concurred, saying that the "...flesh of a Moose in good condition, contains more nourishment than that of any other Deer...even of the Bison." Pioneer naturalist Ernest Thompson Seton wrote: "What the Buffalo was to the Plains, the White-tail Deer to the Southern woods, and the Caribou to the Barrens, the Moose is to this great Northern belt of swamp and timberland...It is the creature that enables the natives to live."

Bull moose have pronounced "bells" on their throats

ging and development create new pockets of whitetail habitat in northern forests, and as whitetails become increasingly common in the forested river valleys of the Rockies, meningeal brainworm may spread. Meningeal brainworm has always been limited to eastern North America because its snail host doesn't thrive on the dry plains. That may change now since game ranchers freely ship ungulates from brainworm country all over the continent.

Moose Hunting

The romantic image of the moose hunter clad in buckskin, slipping silently by canoe along a wooded lakeshore while imitating the rutting call of a moose with a birchbark cone doesn't translate well to the Rocky Mountains. Most moose hunters in the Rockies hunt on foot either by tracking moose in snow or glassing from vantage points that overlook beaverpond complexes or willow-choked stream bottoms. Moose calling, however, can be effective during the October rut.

The Shiras' moose that are most widespread in the Rockies are smaller than Alaska moose or those found in parts of northern Canada. Most moose hunters are not after trophies so much as they are seeking food—up to 600 pounds of excellent, healthy meat. Moose are the largest game animal in the West, however, and a successful hunter can look forward to a day or two of serious work if his prey falls more than a few hundred yards from a handy road.

Roast Snout?

October 19.

We fell in with an Indian hunter and his family...We traded with them for some beaver meat and moose noses; the latter is the most delicate eating I ever met with, and is valued amongst the Indians among all other food.

Paul Kane, 1859
Wanderings of An Artist
(describing a wilderness journey in 1846)

Caribou *(Rangifer tarandus)*

Mountain caribou in Jasper National Park, Alberta

Most people think of caribou as Arctic tundra animals. It's true that most of the world's surviving caribou, and all the largest herds, live in the Far North. Caribou are cold-adapted animals that prefer mild summers and cold winters. Small bands of woodland and mountain caribou, however, forage in the shadow of old-growth forests as far south as northern Idaho and Washington. Most surviving southern herds are endangered.

In the Rocky Mountains, caribou occupied the North Fork of the Flathead River in British Columbia and Montana until the early 1900s. The small herds were vulnerable to hunters and dependent on old-growth forests of spruce and fir. By the 1930s very few survived -- and in 1936 a vast fire swept through the North Fork and destroyed most of their habitat. Caribou are now only memories in a landscape noted for its grizzly bears -- animals that thrive after fire.

Farther west, a few dwindling bands of caribou still range the southern Selkirk Mountains in British Columbia and Idaho. Their habitat continues to fall to chainsaws, however, because of reluctance by forest services to protect old growth reserves. Others die in winter as roadkill when they lick salt on Canada's Highway 3 between Salmo and Creston.

As logging fragments the mountain forests, populations of deer, elk and moose increase in the shrubby second growth. The growing number of other ungulates sustains larger predator populations than would normally live in this deep-snow country. Caribou are vulnerable to mountain lions and wolves, so the logging of their habitat is a double whammy -- it reduces their habitat and increases their predators.

Throughout Alberta and British Columbia, caribou herds are vanishing as the last old-growth habitats are milled into lumber or processed into wood pulp. Unlike other ungulates that thrive on the

Left: Woodland caribou bull

shrubs and greenery that sprout after the chainsaws depart, caribou depend on old-growth conifer forest both for food and shelter. Caribou eat the hanging, hairlike lichens that grow slowly on the branches of old trees. The forest canopy also intercepts snowfall that would otherwise accumulate on the ground and hamper their movements.

Even so, caribou adapt readily to human activity. In fact, they seem disarmingly naive. Loggers often see the ghostlike creatures at the edges of clearcuts, browsing on forage brought down by the chainsaws. Freshly-logged forest is a food bonanza for caribou because it gives them access to the entire tree canopy and all its lichens. Unfortunately, it is a bonanza that will not return for more than a century. By that time -- unless governments act decisively to protect what little caribou habitat remains - many southern caribou herds will have followed the Flathead's herd into oblivion.

Caribou biologists generally agree that closing forest roads and stopping the logging of old-growth forests offer the only long-term hope for the grey ghosts of the northern mountains.

Mountain caribou yearling

Caribou Facts

Length:
bulls: 125-175 cm. (4-5.5 ft.)
cows: 100-150 cm. (3.5-5 ft.)
Weight:
bulls: 110-270 kg. (250-600 lbs.)
cows: 70-160 kg. (150-350 lbs)
Description:
Pale brown or grayish brown animals about the size of a large deer. The neck is paler than the back. Caribou are short-legged, blocky animals with large hooves. Both bulls and cows have antlers, with most of the antler extending backward and palmate brow tines reaching forward over the animal's thick, straight nose. Caribou antlers have widened or "palmate" ends. Calves are reddish brown or pale brown, unspotted, with a blackish stripe down the back. Caribou seem almost to float when they run. They have a distinctive, bouncing trot.
Life Span:
Rarely, twenty years. Most caribou die before the age of ten.
Reproduction:
First breed at forty months of age, or as early as sixteen months under ideal conditions. Cows have a single calf. Twins are very rare.
Food:
Lichens, sedges, forbs and woody browse.
Distribution:
The arctic and coniferous forest regions of northernmost Europe, Asia and North America. Caribou range south as far as the Selkirk Mountains in the northern tip of Idaho. They survive in the Rockies as far south as northern Banff National Park.

Right: Woodland caribou cow

Afterword

I t has taken Nature millions of years to give shape and meaning to the deer, elk, moose and caribou. Her tools were, and still are, the elements of their living environment: hungry predators, green vegetation, hard winters, freedom, weather and wildness.

Summer droughts hone their intimate knowledge of landscapes as relentlessly as do deep winter snows and soft spring rains.

And so, over countless centuries, they have become what they are. Finely-honed senses of smell and hearing help them communicate, detect danger, and find food. Bright eyes watch alertly for predators. Hair-trigger reflexes react to sudden danger. Powerful bodies and time-tested behaviors buy safety for the most fit. Those less perfect fall prey to predators, weather or disease.

The environment that gives shape to these highly-tuned animals, however, has changed. Until the past few decades, no deer, elk or moose had ever seen a road, town, farm, ranch, park or shopping mall. Increasingly, now, these shape the nature of wild ungulates as much as they influence us.

In the future, even more than today, human choices will dominate almost every aspect of ungulates' lives. Their search for forage and shelter will depend on where we choose to log or farm and how we choose to raise livestock. When drought comes, we will control most of the water. Each fall they will migrate to winter ranges that humans own. What happens on that private property will determine whether, and how, they survive. Their habitat will be only as rich and as wild as we allow.

Elk and moose need wolves; deer need cougars and coyotes—and we determine where and under what terms those predators will survive. Where we fail to tolerate predators, disease flourishes and ungulates grow lazy. Without four-legged predators to weed out the weak, wildlife agencies must find a way for human hunters to take up the slack. Humans, however, don't choose the sick or the small. Our hunting

Deer and elk must survive in a world shaped by people

techniques select for different prey behaviors. Human predation has a role to play—but it is no substitute for the wolf, mountain lion, bear or coyote.

Hunting is an honorable pastime, when practiced with integrity and respect. No other cultural activity brings humans into such intimate contact with, and understanding of, nature. Historically, human predators played an important role in helping to shape the nature of these animals we so admire. But when modern hunters rely on roads, bait or technology to cheat our prey, we violate the ancient compact between human predator and hoofed prey. Ethical restraint and fair play have become more important now than ever before to human hunters. These determine whether hunting—

Bull elk bugling during the autumn rut

as predation is meant to do—will make both us and the animals we hunt better creatures. As practised by too many, hunting often does just the opposite.

Substituting birth control for predation artificializes deer and elk. In the same way, feeding ungulates—whether at a backyard bird feeder, a commercial shooting camp or a winter wildlife refuge—steals wildness from animals whose nature it is to be wild. If we allow native animals to become domestic livestock on private land and confine the last wild herds to parks, winter feedgrounds and private hunting reserves, then no longer will we have real elk, deer or moose. Wildness can neither be counterfeited nor contained.

It can, however, be restored. Nothing obliges us to perpetuate past mistakes in wildlife and land management.

For better or worse, the North American west has changed forever. It has become increasingly difficult—but perhaps never more essential—to hang onto what wildness survives and to restore as much as possible of what has been lost.

One of our greatest challenges in the 21st century may be to find a way to live well in a challenging, changing land. We who profess to love the west can only sustain its fundamental nature—and ours—if we succeed in keeping most of it as wild, free, and natural as can be. Part of the measure of our success will be what becomes of the exquisite wild ungulates whose home places we are privileged to share—and doomed, apparently, to control.

May we prove worthy of them.

Reference

Where to Find Them & How to See Them

Elk, deer and moose are where you find them. That can be any of innumerable wild places in the West. The following list is only a sampler of some more accessible or better known viewing locations.

Most national forests and, in Canada, provincial forest reserves are open-access public lands containing abundant summer habitat for native wildlife. In winter ungulates often congregate on private or controlled-access public lands visible from major highways.

Generally, it is easier to spot ungulates in winter when they congregate on winter ranges than in summer when they are more dispersed. However, they are more vulnerable to disturbance during the winter starvation season. In winter the ethical choice is to watch animals from a distance rather than risk forcing them to waste precious energy fleeing from human encroachment.

Ungulates are crepuscular, which means they are most active around dawn and dusk. The best times to look for them, then, are the times of day when people are least likely to be afield.

Good binoculars help both to bring distant animals closer and to compensate for poor light conditions during the magic hours of daybreak and evening. Binoculars do not all have the same light-gathering capability. Choose a pair where the second number is at least five times higher than the first number (eg.: 7X35 or 8X40). A spotting scope with a solid tripod or window mount can also help with distant observations and methodical searching of mountain slopes.

Wildlife Viewing Tips

Take advantage of early morning and late evening when animals are most active. Overcast days with light rain or snow can also be productive.

In winter, ungulates often feed in the open after major storms, even in midday.

Remember: they're watching for you, because to most ungulates humans are predators. Move very slowly, make no sound, and spend a lot of time sitting still and watching.

Feeding areas and waterholes are good places to sit still, using vegetation to break up your silhouette, and watch for ungulates to come and go.

Pay attention to animal noises. Squirrels, ravens and even chickadees can announce the approach of elk or deer.

Use optical equipment -- binoculars and spotting scope—to avoid the need to approach too close to animals. The best wildlife observations are of undisturbed animals, unaware of the fact that they're being watched.

Get out and wander. Even if you don't see wild ungulates, you can learn a lot from following their game trails, finding their feeding sign or, in winter, tracking them.

Set high ethical standards of personal behavior—wild ungulates have enough difficulty surviving without being crowded or unnecessarily disturbed by naturalists or hunters. When you let your choices modify the behavior of a wild animal, you cease to be a sensitive observer and begin to be a problem.

NEW MEXICO

El Malpais National Monument
505 783-4774
Fall through spring: Elk and mule deer are best seen in the Chain of Craters and West Malpais Wildernesses. A good hike is into the Ponderosa pine country of Hole in the Wall. Glassing rimrock areas should produce sightings of mule deer and could also yield a glimpse of mountain lion or coyotes, their chief predators here.

Sargent/Humphries
North of Chama
505 756-2585
Summer and fall: elk and mule deer are abundant and visible.

Fort Bayard
East of Silver City
505 538-2771
Year-round: Coues whitetail—a small southwestern subspecies—live in the pinyon and oak country and can be seen sometimes near dawn and dusk. Mule deer are often visible from the road or along the Cameron Creek trail. Watch for elk in winter.

COLORADO

Arapaho National Wildlife Refuge
Year-round: watch for moose, mule deer and elk in the riparian meadows and open woodlands along the Illinois River. The best viewing area is south of the Refuge, from a ridge next to Forest Road 750, southeast of Rand.

Rocky Mountain National Park
Estes Park, CO 80517-8397
970 586-1206;
www.nps.gov/romo/
Fall and Winter: Moraine Park, Horseshoe Park, Beaver Meadows: mostly elk, also mule deer
Summer: the above, and Trail Ridge Road: mostly elk. Colorado River riparian meadows: moose

Silver Thread Scenic Byway
Self-guided: drive from South Fork to Lake City over Spring Creek Pass, along State Highway 149.
Fall and winter: elk feed in open meadows at dawn and dusk in the Coller State Wildlife Area. Watch for moose in riparian willow thickets along the Rio Grande River and Clear Creek
Summer: moose in the river bottoms; mule deer almost anywhere.

WYOMING

Yellowstone National Park
Box 168
Yellowstone National Park, WY 82190
307 344-7381;
www.nps.gov/yell/
Winter and Spring: elk congregate in the thousands on the Yellowstone northern range, in the Yellowstone and Lamar valleys. Both elk and the wolves that prey on them are highly visible during this season. Road access is limited, however.
Summer: Hayden and Lamar valleys remain productive places for viewing elk, deer and their predators. An early morning or late evening drive may also reveal small bands of elk or deer in high elevation meadows, in the riparian zones along park rivers, in the lush regrowth where the 1988 wildfires burned, or along the edges of geyser basins.

Grand Teton National Park
P.O. Drawer 170
Moose, WY 83012-0170
307 739-3600;
www.nps.gov/grte/
Summer: Float trips or hiking along the Green River offer unparalleled viewing opportunities for elk, mule deer and Shiras moose.

National Elk Refuge
Box C
Jackson, WY 83001
307 733-9212
Open: year round (restricted access)
Winter: up to 15,000 elk congregate in open grasslands and hillsides. Public sleigh rides along the elk feeding lines offer closeup viewing opportunities. Bison and mule deer are also visible.

MONTANA

Blackfoot-Clearwater Wildlife Management Area
40 km. ENE of Missoula on State Highway 200
Open: May 15 to November 15
Winter viewing from Clearwater Junction
Up to 1000 elk and 1500 mule and white-tailed deer winter in the WMA's meadows and open forests. In summer, when controlled public access is permitted, deer occupy the WMA but most elk are at higher elevations in the nearby Bob Marshall Wilderness. Other Wildlife Management Areas are scattered along the Rocky Mountain Front north and east of the Blackfoot-Clearwater and all provide good winter viewing opportunities from their boundaries for elk and mule deer.

National Bison Refuge
Between Missoula and Kalispell on US Hwy 93.
Winter: numerous mule deer and elk winter within sight of the highway.

Waterton-Glacier International Peace Park

Canada: Waterton Lakes National Park
Waterton Park, Alberta T0K 2M0
403 859-2224;
www.parkscanada.gc.ca/

U.S.A.: Glacier National Park
West Glacier, MT. 59936
406 888-5441;
www.nps.gov/glac/
Open: Year round (some roads, including Chief Mountain and Going to the Sun

Highways, closed in winter)
Winter: up to 1200 elk, hundreds of whitetails and smaller numbers of mule deer congregate in the lower Waterton River valley. Mule deer are common in the Waterton townsite and sometimes cougars hunt them there. Summer: elk are at higher elevations but sometimes appear along the Going to the Sun Road, especially in evenings. Look for whitetails along the Chief Mountain Highway and in the Apgar area.

ALBERTA

Banff, Jasper, Yoho and Kootenay National Parks
Banff National Park
Banff, Alberta T0L 0C0
Open: year round
Winter: watch for elk and mule deer, and occasional whitetails, along the north sides of the lower Athabasca and Bow Rivers. Elk are scarce in the Kicking Horse River valley and common in Kootenay River valleys, where whitetails may also appear along the roadsides at dusk. Travelers on the Icefields Parkway sometimes see caribou near Sunwapta Falls. Wolves and coyotes hunt wild ungulates along the major river valleys.
Summer: Elk, mule deer and moose are less common near the highways, but try an evening drive in the lower Bow valley. A good hiking destination for mule deer, moose, elk and occasional caribou is Jasper's Opal Hills trail near Maligne Lake.

Elk Island National Park
Year round: white-tailed deer, elk and moose can be spotted

almost anywhere, along with free-roaming bison.

Places to Learn About Elk and Deer

Rocky Mountain Elk Foundation
Wildlife Visitor Center
2291 - W. Broadway
Missoula, MT
(800) 225-5355

Boone and Crockett Club National Headquarters
250 - Station Drive
Missoula, MT 59801-2753
(406) 542-1888

National Park Summer Institute Programs:

Glacier Institute
Glacier Natural History Association
Box 1457
Kalispell, Montana 59903

The Jasper Institute
Parks and People, Jasper
Box 100
Jasper, Alberta T0E 1E0

Heritage Education Program
Waterton Natural History Association
Box 145
Waterton Park, Alberta

Calendar of Programs

Twice a year the bi-weekly Colorado-based High Country News publishes special issues that list conservation education and outdoor programs available across the Rocky Mountain West. More information: www.hcn.org/

T0K 2M0
www.lis.ab.ca/wnha/

Yellowstone Institute
Field Courses and Nature Study Vacations
Box 117
Yellowstone National Park, WY 82190
(307) 344-2294

Teton Science School
Box 68T
Kelly, WY 83011
(307) 733-4765
www.tetonscience.org

Conservation Resources

Wildlife Management Agencies

CANADA

Alberta Ministry of Environmental Protection
Fish and Wildlife Division
Main Floor, 9945-108th Street,
Edmonton, AB T5K 2G6

Useful Web Sites

Deer of the World:
www.deer.rr.ualberta.ca/
Links to elk websites:
www.iup.edu/~ferenc/elk000a9.htm
Hunting seasons: www.buckmasters.com/hunting_seasons/
DeerNet:
cervid.forsci.ualberta.ca/
Links to wildlife sites:
www.gorp.com/gorp/activity/wildlife.htm
Web links to more Conservation Groups:
www.enviro-source/us/
us15.htm-community.web.net/
ecoweb/ecoorglist.html

British Columbia Ministry of Environment, Lands and Parks
Wildlife Branch
2nd floor, 10470 - 152 Street
Surrey, B.C. V3R 0Y3

Manitoba Ministry of Natural Resources
Wildlife Branch
Legislative Building
Winnipeg, MB R3C 0V8

Saskatchewan Ministry of Environment and Resource Management
Fish and Wildlife Branch
3211 - Albert Street
Regina, SK S4S 5W6

Ministry of Renewable Resources
Government of Yukon Territory
Box 2703
Whitehorse, YK Y1A 2C6

UNITED STATES

Alaska Department of Fish and Game
Box 25526
Juneau, AK 99802-5526

Zippy Way to Say It

You want to let your elected representatives know your views about ungulate conservation, game ranching or habitat— but you don't know how to find them. No problem. If you live in the U.S.A., just visit www.vox-pop.org/zipper/ on the World Wide Web. This web site prompts you for your zip code and then tells you the email and postal address of your congress person or senator. Canadians can go to www.earth-net.net/pac/canada/federal/index.html

Arizona Game & Fish Department
2221 W. Greenway Rd.
Phoenix, AZ 85023-4399

Colorado Division of Wildlife
6060 Broadway
Denver, CO 80216

Idaho Department of Fish and Game
Box 25
Boise, ID 83707

Montana Fish, Wildlife and Parks
1420 - E. 6th Avenue
Helena, MT 59620

Nevada Division of Wildlife
1100 Valley View Road
Reno, Nevada

New Mexico Department of Game and Fish
PO Box 25112
Santa Fe, NM 87504

Oregon Department of Fish and Wildlife
Box 59
Portland, OR 97207

Wyoming Game & Fish Dept.
5400 Bishop Blvd.
Cheyenne, WY 82006

Utah Division of Wildlife
1596 W. North Temple
Salt Lake City, Utah 84116

Conservation Organizations

CANADA

Canadian Parks and Wilderness Society
1019 -4th Ave. SW

Calgary, Alberta T2P 0K8

Canadian Wildlife Federation
2740 Queensview Drive
Ottawa, Ontario K2B 1A2

Rocky Mountain Elk Foundation
Box 940
Rocky Mountain House, Alberta T0M 1T0

The Nature Conservancy of Canada
794A Broadview Avenue
Toronto, Ontario M4K 2P7

Sierra Club of Canada
412-1 Nicholas St.
Ottawa, Ontario, K1N 7B7

World Wildlife Fund Canada
90 Eglinton Avenue East, Suite 504
Toronto, Ontario M4P 2Z7

UNITED STATES

Boone and Crockett Club
250 - Station Drive
Missoula, MT 59801-2753

Defenders of Wildlife
1244 - 19th Street NW
Washington, D.C. 20036

Isaac Walton League of America
707 Conservation Lane
Gaithersburg, MD 20875

Land Trust Alliance
1319 F Street NW
Washington, DC 20004-1106

National Audubon Society
700 Broadway
New York, NY 10003

National Parks and
Conservation Association
1776 Massachusetts Avenue,
N.W.
Washington, DC 22036

National Wildlife
Federation
1400- 16th Street NW
Washington DC 20036

The Nature Conservancy
1815 - North Lynn Street
Arlington, VA 22209

Orion—The Hunters
Institute
P.O. Box 5088
Helena, MT 59604

Rocky Mountain
Elk Foundation
2291 W. Broadway
Missoula, MT 59802-1813

Sierra Club
85 Second St., Second Floor
San Francisco,CA 94105-3441

The Wilderness Society
900 - 17th Street NW
Washington DC 20006

World Wildlife Fund U.S.
1250 - 24th Street N.W.
Washington DC 20037-1175

Selected Readings

Books

Geist V. 1991. Elk Country.
NorthWord Press, Minocqua
WI. ISBN 1-5597-1128-0

Geist V. 1991. Mule Deer
Country. Western Producer
Prairie Books, Saskatoon SK.
ISBN 0-88833-
349-8

Halls L.K. (ed.) 1984. White-
tailed Deer: Ecology and Management. Wildlife Manage-
ment Institute,
Stackpole Books, Harrisburg,
PA. ISBN 0-8117-0486-6.

Kerasote T. 1993. Bloodties:
Nature, Culture, and the Hunt.
Kodansha International, New
York NY. ISBN 1-56836-027-4

Leopold, A. 1949. A Sand
County Almanac. Random
House, Toronto, ON. ISBN 0-
345-34505-3.

Nelson R. 1997. Heart and
Blood: Living With Deer in
America. Alfred A. Knopf, New
York, NY. ISBN 0-679-40522-4

Petersen D. 1991. Racks: The
Natural History of Antlers and
the Animals that Wear Them.
Capra Press, Santa Barbara,
CA. ISBN TK

Petersen D. 1998. Elkheart: A
Personal Tribute to Wapiti and
Their World.
Johnson Books, Boulder, CO.
ISBN 1-55566-225-0.

Posewitz J. 1994. Beyond Fair
Chase: The Ethics and Tradition of Hunting. Falcon Press,
Helena, MT. ISBN 1-56044-
283-2.

Russell J. 1998. The Nature of
Caribou. Sierra Club Books,
San Francisco, CA. ISBN 1-
55054-622-8.

Thomas J.W. (ed.) 1982. Elk of
North America: Ecology and
Management. Wildlife Man-
agement Institute, Stackpole
Books, Harrisburg, PA. ISBN 0-
8117-0571-4.

Trefethen J. 1975. An American Crusade for Wildlife. Win-
chester Press, NY. ISBN 0-
87691-207-2

Wallmo O.C. (ed.) 1981. Mule
and Black-tailed Deer of North
America. Wildlife Manage-
ment Institute, University of
Nebraska Press, Lincoln, NE.
ISBN 0-8032-4715-X.

Periodicals

Bugle: Journal of Elk and the
Hunt
2291 - West Broadway
Missoula, MT 59802
www.rmef.org

Wild Outdoor World (chil-
dren's magazine)
P.O Box 8249
Missoula, MT 59807-8249
www.rmef.org

High Country News "A Paper
for People Who Care About the
West"
Box 1090
Paonia, CO 81428
www.hcn.org

Index

A

Alberta, wildlife viewing, 138
antler velvet, 21, 24, 25, 50, 52
antlers, 13, 19-21, 112
    archaelogical findings, 38
    collecting, 20, 21
    decorating with, 21
    ecological value, 21
    trophy, 114
    See also antler velvet; poaching
Araphaho National Wildlife
Refuge, wildlife viewing, 137
art, 21, 22-23
Audubon Society, 33

B

Baker, Dan, 30
Bambi, 28
Bandelier National Monument, 37
Banff National Park
    elk in townsite, 76-77
    wildlife viewing, 138
Bang's disease, 78
Barrett, George, 64
bears, as predators, 27
Beaver, Samson, 49
beavers, 70
Beck, Tom, 52
Bergmann's Rule, 15
bighorn sheep, 19
binoculars, 136
birth control, 135
bison, 19
black-tailed deer, 13-14, 91
Blackfoot-Clearwater Wildlife
Management Area, wildlife
viewing, 137
bobcats, as predators, 28-29
books, recommended, 140
Boone and Crockett Club, 33, 48,
82, 138, 139
brainworm, 128-29
brucellosis, 78
Bull Moose Party, 127

C

call devices, elk bugles, 72
Canadian Conservation Commission, 33
caribou, 131-33
    antlers, 19

diet, 132
distribution, 131, 132
habitat, 132
hooves, 18
impact of logging, 132
life span, 132
physical description, 132
reproduction, 132
taxonomy and origins, 13-14
caribou meat, 92
    See also venison
Caton, John, 109
cattle grazing, 61
cheatgrass, 46
chronic wasting disease (CWD),
104-5
Colorado
    introduction of moose, 123
    wildlife viewing, 137
conservation education, 138
conservation movement, 39-40
conservation organizations
    Canada and U.S., 138, 139-40
    opposition to game farming,
52
    See also names of
organizations
conservation surcharges, 33
cougars, as predators, 77, 101
coyotes, as predators, 27-28

D

Dalman, Dale, 77
Dasmann, William, 101
deer
    in ancient economies, 32, 36,
38
    antlers, 19-21, 24, 112
    digestive system, 24-25, 27
    and dogs, 113
    exploitation and extinction, 39
    feeding, 85, 101, 135
    in frontier times, 38-39
    hair, 31
    hooves, 18
    migration, 31
    milk, 95
    in native myths, 32
    position in food pyramid, 13
    predators of, 25-29
    shields, 110
    species, 14-15, 18
    sterilizing of, 30

    trophy antlers, 114
    web sites, 138
    in winter, 29, 31
deer decoys, 102
deer farming, 48-50, 117
    disease transmission, 79, 81,
104
    opposition from conservation
groups, 52
    velvet antler harvests, 21, 24,
52
deer meat, 45, 92
    See also venison
deer velvet. *See* antler velvet
diseases
    in deer, 104-5, 128-29
    in elk, 75, 78-79, 81, 128
    in moose, 128-29
    See also names of diseases
dogs, and deer, 113

E

Edgerton, Doug, 65
El Malpais National Monument,
136
elk, 55-87
    aggressive behavior, 76-77
    antlers, 19
    coexistence with ranchers, 81-
83, 85
    communication among, 72-73
    confusion over names, 59
    defensive behavior, 60, 63, 64,
70, 71
    diet, 56, 58-60
    digestive system, 24-25, 27
    diseases and parasites, 75, 78-
79, 81, 128
    distribution, 56
    exploitation and extinction,
39, 58, 59
    feedgrounds, 85, 135
    habitat, 58, 61, 63, 65, 70, 76-
77, 82-83, 86
    hair, 31
    hooves, 18
    Irish, 12
    kinds of, 57
    life span, 56
    logging and roads, 61, 65, 66
    migration, 31
    and Native Americans, 32, 56-
58

physical description, 56
position in food pyramid, 13
predators of, 27-28, 77
reproduction, 56, 60, 65, 70
rutting season, 71-72
sterilizing of, 30
taxonomy and origins, 13-14, 55
teeth, 59
in urban areas, 76-77
web sites, 138
in winter, 29, 31, 74-75
elk bugles, 72
Elk Island National Park
predators, 37
wildlife viewing, 138
elk meat, 45
See also venison

F
farmers and ranchers
coexistence with elk, 81-83, 85
coexistence with mule deer, 105
compensation programs, 43
and hunters, 41, 43-44, 86
fawns, 97, 110-11
feedgrounds, 85, 101, 135
fencing, 41, 43
Fisher, Brian, 25
flytying, using deer hair, 31
folk art, use of antlers, 21
food pyramid, 13
forest fires
ecological role, 37, 41, 63, 75, 121
setting by native tribes, 38, 63
Fort Bayard, 136
Fort Collins, 30

G
game farming. *See* deer farming
Garcia, Andrew, 32
Gartshore, Mary, 116
Gayton, Don, 46
Geist, Valerius, 12, 15, 19, 40, 90, 98, 103
Glacier National Park, wildlife viewing, 137-38
Glickman, Dan, 65
goats, horns, 19
government agencies, Canada and U.S., 138-39
Grand Canyon, 94
Grand Teton National Park, wildlife viewing, 137

Grey, Zane, 94
Grinnell, George Bird, 33, 42, 48
ground squirrels, 63

H
habitat
caribou, 132
elk, 58, 61, 63, 65, 70, 76-77, 82-83, 86
moose, 119-22
mule deer, 92
white-tailed deer, 107, 109-10
habitat conservation, 50-52, 66-67, 82-83, 86, 94
Hansen, Milo, 114
Haskins, Jim, 62, 103
Haskins, Robert, 51
herding, 71
Hewitt, C. Gordon, 33
hooves, 18
Hornaday, William, 33, 41, 63, 117
horns, 19
Hoskin, Robert, 85
hunt farms, 50
hunter-conservationists, 33, 40, 42-43
hunting, 83, 134-35
canned hunts, 50
conservation surcharges, 33
controversy over, 48
deer, 108, 115, 117
during elk rut, 72, 86
ecological effect, 36
end of market-hunting, 33
moose, 129
on private land, 41, 43-44, 86, 115
ranch, 51
regulations, 40, 108
technological gadgets, 45
trophy, 114, 117
web sites, 138
white-tailed deer, 113
See also hunter-conservationists; Orion
hydatid tapeworm, 79

I
Ice Age, 12
internet sites, 138, 139
Irish elk, 12

K
Kaibab National Forest, 94
Kane, Paul, 129

Kerasote, Ted, 30, 44
Kirkpatrick, Jay, 30
knapweed, 46

L
leafy spurge, 46
Leopold, Aldo, 29, 43, 45, 85
liver fluke, 78-79
livestock, disease transmission, 78, 79, 81
logging
impact on caribou, 132
impact on elk, 61
Love, Bob, 50
lungworm, 79
Lutts, Ralph, 28

M
mad cow disease, 104-5
McCabe, Richard and Thomas, 39
Mech, Dave, 112
meningeal brainworm, 128-29
migration, 31
mineral licks, 60
Montana, wildlife viewing, 137-38
moose, 119-29
antlers, 19
confusion over names, 59
defensive behavior, 122
diet, 120
digestive system, 24-25, 27
distribution, 119, 120
habitat, 119-22
hair, 31
hooves, 18
impact of wildfires, 121
introduction into Colorado, 123
kinds of, 119, 122
life span, 120
migration, 31
physical description, 120
reproduction, 120, 122
stag-moose, 14
taxonomy and origins, 13-14
in winter, 29
moose meat, 45
See also venison
Morgantini, Luigi, 64
mountain lions, as predators, 26-27, 81
mule deer, 89-105
aggressive behavior, 98
antlers, 19
coexistence with ranchers and farmers, 105